THE VIRTUAL WORKPLACE

One Size Doesn't Fit All

State-of-the-Art Institute
November 7-8, 1996
Washington, DC

1997
Special Libraries Association

Some articles and material included in this publication are reprinted with permission from works copyrighted by other publishers. See individual articles for copyright statements.

© 1997 by Special Libraries Association
1700 Eighteenth Street, NW
Washington, DC 20009-2514
1-202-234-4700
www.sla.org

Note: To preserve original wording and format used in the presentations, these papers were compiled *exactly* as submitted by the writers and/or presenters. SLA is not responsible for any editorial errors within this text.

Contents

Introduction

By Valerie Taylor

Director, Professional Development

Special Libraries Association

.

Have you ever wondered how you'll spend your work day in the year 2000? Has the growth in technology impacted how you communicate with your colleagues and clients? The 1996 State-of-the-Art Institute, *The Virtual Workplace, One Size Doesn't Fit All,* explored how the nature of work is changing, and how organizations and information professionals must prepare for the change.

The increasing use of new technology has given birth to the concept of "virtuality." As information specialists, many special librarians are familiar with terms and concepts such as virtual offices, virtual classrooms, and virtual open-houses. As the technology that allows us to experiment with these concepts becomes increasingly popular, it won't be long before we all operate in a virtual workplace, in fact, some companies are already experimenting with the idea. Many organizations are adopting telecommuting policies which will allow employees to work from their homes, Internet shopping is expected to triple in the next five years, and universities have begun offering graduate degree courses on the World Wide Web.

The SLA State-of-the-Art Institute, November 7-8, 1996 in Washington, DC, featured leading experts in technology, human resources, information science, and business who discussed emerging trends already shaping the way business is conducted around the world.

Opening speaker David Hakken, Ph.D., president of the Society for the Anthropology of Work, brought a unique anthropological perspective to the virtual workplace discussing the notion of decoupling workspace from workplace. Participants also heard case studies from professionals who have made the transition to virtual workplaces. Eric Richert, Sun Microsystems, explores the role of the workplace in increasing productivity and the cost savings in this equation, and discusses why, in the virtual workplace, one size doesn't fit all. Velda Ruddock, TBWA Chiat/Day, describes her agency's concept of the virtual workplace and how her department provides intelligence in this progressive organization's corporate environment. Linda McFadden, an independent consultant, provides an overview of specific areas of activity involved in the unfolding of a new work order. In addition, Judith J. Field, Wayne State University, presents an overview of the evolution of the virtual organization and the adaption of library services to this new environment. Joy Park, McKinsey & Co, compares knowledge management in two very different corporations contrasting the role played by their respective information centers in initiating, structuring, or managing their organization's knowledge. Patricia A. Frame, Strategies for Human Resources, highlights the benefits and challenges of flexiwork and what is needed to make this work option successful.

In addition to the excellent presentations by the State-of-the-Art Institute speakers, a variety of relevant articles on the virtual workplace is included in this publication. With the many challenges and opportunities the virtual workplace brings information professionals, "Competencies for Special Librarians of the 21st Century," has also been included. This report describes, in detail, the competencies that will prepare information professionals for the next decade and beyond, encompassing knowledge, understanding, skills and attitudes. And finally, Institute speaker Linda McFadden has graciously compiled an extensive bibliography of resources on the topic to help further study.

The Virtual Workplace: Decoupling Space from Place

by Dr. David Hakken
Professor of Anthropology and Director, Policy Center
State University of New York Institute of Technology at Utica/Rome
President, Society for the Anthropology of Work
American Anthropological Association

Prepared for the Annual State-of-the-Art Institute,
Special Libraries Association, Washington, D.C.
11/7-8/96

1. Introduction

1.1 Virtual Work Ethnography in Silicon Valley

For some fifteen years now, I have been a cyberspace work ethnographer. That is, I am among those using field methods to study the future of work, simultaneously observing and participating in the use of the computer-based advanced information technologies (AITs) that most of us in contemporary societies believe are changing our lives (Hakken 1993a; l993b; forthcoming). Charles Darrah, an anthropologist similarly engaged at Cal State San Jose--in the belly of the cyberspace monster, so to speak--tells a poignant story (1995) which helps frame this opening presentation on the "virtual" workspace of the future. His project was to try to understand what it was like to be part of a Silicon Valley family whose relationships were extensively mediated by computer-dependent electronic devices, such as pagers. Like any good ethnographer, Darrah's approach was to get his informants, the family members, together to have a conversation about what difference the modemed lap-top computers, mobile telephones, dedicated chat groups, as well as the pagers, etc. made. His main problem, however, was finding a time when Mom, Dad, Sister Sue and Brother Bob were all in one place. For several of these-- shall we call them, "virtual?"--families, the interview was the first time in a month they had all been in the same place together!

On the surface, Darrah's is not a story not about work. Still, the "adult cyborg units" in Darrah's informant sample were employed by organizations which had provided the pagers, modems, etc. "free," as "benefits" of the job. the trade off was that employees were essentially "on call" at any time of the day, night, or week. "Virtually" anywhere had become a workspace, and boundaries between home and work, private and public, the personal and the political, were dissolving rapidly.

1.2 Virtual Work and Social Evolution

If such conditions were to become general, it would mean the reversal of a very important social development in the history of commodity-based employment or "industrial" social formations. In the largely rural 19th Century, the family farm was both home and workplace for most Americans. The separation off of the physical workplace from the home to the workshop, factory, or office was a major social change, an important part of the transformation of "organic work" into "alienated labor." We might optimistically see the development Darrah chronicles as the reintegration of the home and work; this is one way to apprehend the network-linked home office, the notion of "virtual work" perhaps most familiar to us. More negatively, we could see such developments as the appear to Gideon Kunda, author of 1993's *Engineering Culture*, a pun of a book title which is arguably the decade's most sinister. Kunda describes the more or less systematic breakdown of any boundary between the corporate and personal lives of the professional workers at "Tech," a Route 128 corridor high tech firm which looks considerably like the Digital Equipment Corporation. He wonders about the implications for democracy of a society who's most privileged workers can no longer distinguish between their personal values and those of the corporate cultures for which they work.

1.3 Virtual Work and the Decoupling of Space from Place

My subtitle--the decoupling of space from place--suggests another, both less politicized and more generally accurate way to describe the cumulative effect of the range of social developments already associated with the spread of advanced information technology (AIT). That is, the more we use AIT, the more tenuous the connections of our activities to particular places. We occupy "workspaces" rather than workplaces with a single locus in space. Even when we share a physical space with co-workers, our attention is increasingly drawn to other times or places, other "spaces" constructed mostly in the minds of those with whom we interact, whether on the telephone, in the video-conference, through the list-serve, the chat group, the professional association, the "team" with members from multiple "networked" organizations, and so on.

When applying the modifier "virtual" to work, we might have in mind something relatively narrow, like the organization with several people working at home. Somewhat perversely, we might stress the implied contrast between "virtual" and IRL (in real life) work, as when we wonder about whether all that time clanging on the keys actually leads to anything concrete. For this Institute, however, I challenge you to think of "virtual work" in the third way I have been trying to name, to use the term as a useful descriptor of what work may well be generally like in the future, in cyberspace. I suggest to you that we can count on cyberwork being increasingly less bound to physical, "real" places and their concreteness, more dependent upon the shared imaginings of "once were" humans (whom I will call cyborgs) whose interactions are increasingly mediated by clever machines. (Notice I did not say "intelligent.") Conceived thusly, "virtual work" becomes a reasonable label under which to conceptualize what is likely to happen to workspace relations in particular and social relations in general as we enter cyberspace.

1.4 Today's objectives

In sum, I have three objectives in mind when asking you to accompany me on the following anthropological "walkabout" in virtual workspace:
.   like any good keynote, to provoke you, by, among other things, "talking that (cyber)talk";
.   to demonstrate use of a notion, the accelerating decoupling of workspace from workplace, as a means to organize our thoughts regarding work and social life more broadly as we move into the future, because this notion captures both continuities and

discontinuities, a strong sense of both being necessary if we are to discipline effectively our imaginings; and

. to equip us intellectually for the daunting task of co-colonizing this cyber-world at the same time as we co-invent it.

2. The Work Anthropology Perspective

2.1 Evolutionary Perspective

I feel compelled to add few further introductory words regarding the somewhat peculiar way work anthropologists think about work. For example, we tend to think in evolutionary terms, being sensitive to how the basic arrangements among humans for obtaining what the need have changed through time, have become increasingly mediated by other social relationships--the wage relationship, or entities, like communication technology--for example. We also like to approach things cross-culturally. I've studied computer-mediated work in Sheffield, England, Oslo, Norway, and Stockholm, Sweden, as well as here in the United States.

2.2 Ethnographic Perspective

Work anthropologists generally chose to study work ethnographically, to learn by doing and by asking a lot of questions. When ethnographers write, we generally tell stories, and enough of us have read Foucault, Derrida, and other "Post-modernists" to create a full-blown crisis between those who still wish our stories to still be considered "objective," the stuff of science, and those who don't.

My own view is that we must find a way to be both scientific and relevant, both intellectually and socially. The issues we confront as we transition from Modern Society to whatever is coming are so important that, however complex, difficult, and likely to be misunderstood, we ethnographers have a special obligation to show how thinking about them can be grounded in concrete social contexts--that is, to be empirical. At the same time, our ethnography must have something to say to the most serious issues we face if it is to have a legitimate claim on social wealth.

Thus, I do "the ethnography of the future" by studying those in the present--members of housing estate computer clubs in Sheffield, quadriplegic users of voice-activated computers in Utica, information system developers in Norway, denizens of cyber-cafe's in Stockholm--whose experience is likely to be suggestive of more general future social dynamics. Teaching in a technological branch of a state university has meant that, in an important sense, I am always doing field work in "really existing" proto-cyberspace. It has also meant I have had the opportunity to do both basic and applied research and even practice, to range from abstract questions about the cultural construction of computing in the Nordic countries to building software which uses eye movement to control immediate environments.

3. A Cyberspace Ethnography Primer

I am completing a book which I intend to call _Cyborgs@Cyberspace: The Ethnography of the Future?_ The book is intended as a "state of the art" summary of cyberspace ethnography--what we cybernauts know, what we don't, and what we should be thinking about. Like those who study gatherer/hunters or peasants, one thing we cyber-ethnographers need if we are to make sense to each other, let alone others, is a shared way of speaking. As a left-handed way to justify my rather "shi-shi" book title, as well as some of the odder forms of speech which I used in telling Darrah's Silicon Valley story, I now offer a demi-explication of the following concepts discussed in the book:

3.1. Computer Revolution

By "Computer Revolution," I mean the widely-shared idea that we in the "developed" world are living/have lived through a fundamental social transformation. Further, this social revolution has been induced by computer-mediated activity (CMA), the development and use of the electronic computer.

A CR is certainly possible and may even be likely at some time in the future. I am unimpressed by those who argue that it has happened already. I suggest that we would do well to avoid mouthing advertising copy and instead find ways to talk about contemporary social change which show greater appreciation for the complex role of technology in it.

3.2. Technology Actor Networks

From interdisciplinary scholarship in Science, Technology, and Society (STS), cyberspace ethnography takes the idea that technologies do not cause social change on their own. Rather, social impacts emerge through networks of machines, organizations, and humans--technology actor networks (TANs). For a TAN, like the automobile/Interstate highway/driver TAN, the most important TAN in the American transportation system, to be come dominant, a vast alliance, a selection from among available design options, and a coming to terms with powerful social forces all must take place. Such dominant TANs evolve slowly, and they may be as conservative as they are transformative.

3.3. Computopian and Compputropian Rhetoric

"Computopians," a term obviously inspired by Thomas More, are those tend to find in each new bell or whistle the answer to basic dilemmas of the human condition--like those who mindlessly celebrate the home office. Alvin and Heidi Toffler tend toward computopianism. "Compputropians," like those who stress the possibilities for alienation in computerized home work, see with each new machine "a grave threat to social life as we know it"; I place Jeremy Rifkin's, *The End of Work* (1995) in this camp. The term itself is inspired by Raymond Williams' concern for the "putrefying" implications of industrial work. Both perspectives tend to presume that a CR has already taken place. Instead, we need to cultivate more skeptical figures of speech which support the production of good empirical data regarding the actual social correlates of each innovation/ and of the broader potential TAN into which it might fit.

3.4. Computer-mediated Activity (CMA) and Computer-mediated Communication (CMC)

"Computer-mediated activity" (CMA) refers to all the things that humans do in which computers play a meaningful part, as in the representation of human labor processes in a computer program. CMA was the initial inspirations for CR rhetoric. More recently,

CR-type talk has been induced by on "computer-mediated communication" (CMC), the increasing use of email, the Internet, and on-line services, but also including the other communications technologies--e.g., cable--now being digitized. It is CMC which is now supposed to "take us to tomorrow."

3.5. Cyberspace: Where CMA meets CMC

Coined by William Gibson in *Neuromancer*, "cyberspace" is the notional "space" which one inhabits while engaged in CMC, whether "surfing the World Wide Web" or negotiation an Apple desktop. Increasingly however, any computer-mediated representation of activity in one place can be communicated anywhere else there is a receiving computer; that is, wherever there is CMA, there is cyberspace. It thus makes sense that, in popular discourse, talk of CRs has been replaced with talk of cyberspace or "the Cyberspace hypothesis." The term "cyberspace" is now used quite generally, to refer to that way of life which at least some people believe is being simultaneously invented and, at least possibly, lived at the intersection of CMA and CMC.

3.6. Cyberians, Cybernauts, and Cyber-prosthetics

To stop here, however, would be to remain thinking of technologies as artifacts, and people as mere life forms. Those creatures living (or trying to live) in cyberspace we can call "Cyberians," while those self-consciously engaged in its exploration we can call "cybernauts." Life in Cyberia, all this CMAing and CMCing, would be impossible without using AIT devices. A strictly biological life form (that is, one around whom an absolute boundary was drawn at the skin), cannot "be" in cyberspace, just as effective movement though a city by a quadriplegic dependent upon a wheel chair is impossible without curb cuts. Hence there is an important analogy to be made between the way Cyberians use computer artifacts and the way many persons with disabilities use prostheses.

3.7. Cyborgs: Inhabitants of Cyberspace (and Everywhere Else!)

From a TAN perspective, most of the actual, key actors in cyberspace are unified techno-bio forms, what long ago in science fiction were called "cyborgs." As opposed to a robot, a strictly mechanical device, a cyborg had at least at one time identifiable biological and mechanical components. Nonetheless, it "functions" as a unit, and any attempt to separate the bio and the mechanico is specious.

3.7.1 Cyborgs as Creoles

In other words, in cyberspace we are all cyborgs. Anthropology can help us understand the implications of this realization. In linguistics, for example, we have languages known as Creoles, which grow out of contacts between, usually, the speech of colonizers and of the colonized. What is distinctive of a Creole is that while it has obvious roots in each of the donor languages, it is not reducible to either; it is its own thing. So Cyborgs are Creolized.

3.7.2 Cyborgs as Objects

To understand cyborgs@cyberspace, we can also get some help from computer science, especially the object-oriented approaches to language and programming so popular at the moment. As a way to modularize programming, such approaches center on the construction of "objects," special computerized representations of things IRL, rather than processes. Among the technical advantages of such an object-orientation is that objects can be programmed with "inheritability" and "synchronicity"; that is, a change in any one representation of the object will automatically result in similar changes in all other networked representations of that object. Object approaches are powerful tools for promoting continuity in de-centralized activities, like a distributed data base.

Each actor cyborg in cyberspace has "object" characteristics and potentials, can be a Creolized object. Cyborgs, like people, are in some ways all the same and in others all unique; the mechanisms to promote similarity/difference are, however, different.

3.7.3 Are People Cyborgs and Cyborgs People?

How significant are the differences between cyborgs@cyberspace and pre-cyberspace "human" units? Neuro-physiology has something to say about this, especially with regard to the displacement of the Cartesian "theater" (Dennett 199). This is a model of human mental processes, articulated by Decartes, in which the central moment of each mental activity is that of individual "consciousness." It turns out that most of our mental processes don't involve consciousness. They go on without sequentially organized, orderly moments of "being aware" of what we are doing. Rather, our brains function like so many information processors linked in parallel, observing, mediating, storing, recalling, and comparing chemically a great deal of information, only some of which, on the odd but important occasion, is raised to "consciousness."

3.7.4 Cyborgs and Computers

Back to anthropology, which suggests a further analogy between a culture and multiple information processors. We think we share with those in our culture the same view of the world, but in fact our cultural constructions, in the words of A.F.C. Wallace (1972), are more mazeways for "muddling through" with diverse meanings than machines for imposing cultural uniformity. A culture is thus more like a brace of networked parallel processes exchanging information than like a shared consciousness. In this regard, all cultures, not just cyberspace, are cyborgic to their core.

Traveling down this conceptual road has obvious implications for general anthropology. Except to indicate that cyberspace ethnography has much to say to all ethnographers, I today set aside further explorations of these implications for today.

3.8. *the decoupling of space from place and the global ecumene*

Finally, I have already suggested that a common thread tying together much of what we cybernauts have "discovered" can be summarized as "the decoupling of space from place." I suggest that this phrase can as well serve as our key to thinking about virtual work.

It is true that the current, cyberspace-related decoupling is more precisely a further stage in a long historical process. In the 19th Century, not only do we find a decoupling of work from home; we also find, as argued by Benedict Anderson in *Imagined Communities* (198), a decoupling of identity from immediate geographic locale. In order to construct viable social formations out of the congeries of individual societies which were the "raw material" of the new nations of the early 19th Century--e.g., the United States--, it was necessary to create a new kind of trans-local identity--e.g., the "American." On Anderson's telling, this collective imaginative act depended heavily on a newish communication technology, the mass circulation newspaper.

3.9 Colonizing Cyberia

As we colonize Cyberia, space is further disengaged from place. Swedish ethnographer Ulf Hannerz (1996) has suggested the phrase "global ecumene" as an alternative to Marshall McLuhan's "global village" for capturing the transnational cultural experience of this current era. The root Greek word "Oikumeme" means "the inhabited world," while the modifier "global" stresses the sense in which contemporary people/cyborgs "inhabit" the globe as a unified entirety. It is quite appropriate, I think, that a Swede--from the most traveled people in the world, the "nation" with the most thoroughly trans-nationalized economy, the producers of arguably the least culturally-distinctive pop music tradition--from ABBA to Roxette--the people in my experience most likely to consider themselves to be "without cultural distinctiveness"--should be our foremost ethnographer of cultural currents which ignore national borders. As we watch our Justice Department's febrile and ultimately feeble efforts to control encryption technology--let alone the Congress's absurd and cynical Communications Decency Act-- who can doubt that cyberspace is the prime "spacus" of the global ecumene?

4. Current Issues in Cyberspace Ethnography

4.1 There has not been a "Computer Revolution"

I hope to have convinced you that cyber-ethnographers have to hand some useful concepts with which to describe and begin to analyze what they find through their fieldwork in proto-cyberspace. I have also suggested at least one meaningful finding, a secular tendency for an accelerated decoupling of space from place. On this finding, cybernauts have turned away from the "Computer Revolution" idea. The reasons for skepticism regarding the CR, for thinking of it as a myth, include the following:

- the virtually universal susceptibility of especially Americans, as in advertising, to facile technological determinist thinking;
- the related, frequent confusion of correlation with causation in CR talk;
- the paucity of good empirical work tracing traces actual connections between contemporary social change and technology use; and
- the rapid burn-out of every supposed AIT related "revolution" thus far; e.g., the computerized teaching machine revolution" of the early 1970s, the "robotics at work" and "home computer" revolutions of the 1980s, etc.

4.1.1 There has been an Acceleration of the Decoupling of Space from Place

The visibly rapid development of CMC has further marginalized CR-talk. All of this has allowed cybernauts to ask better questions: How much does it matter that, in cyberspace, those experiences, especially face-to-face ones, that we used to think of as "real life" are marginalized? Just what are the broad implications of the further decoupling of space from place that we observe in the many different proto-cyberspace venues where AIT is in use?

To cybernauts, these are better questions because:

- the focus is shifted from artifacts to socio-cultural relations, foregrounding socially-constructed spatial rather than alienated technical relations;
- consequently, talk more easily avoids technological deterministic tropes;
- these questions suggest many opportunities for empirical ethnographic work; and
- they make it easier to "ground" discourse along the individual-ecumene continuum.

4.2 some of the General Issues We Cybernauts Argue about Now

This shift in intellectual focus can be illustrated through a list of the kinds of things we cybernauts argue about among ourselves:

. What are the implications of the transition to cyberspace for power relations among people/cyborgs--e.g., what about cyberdemocracy?
. Will cyberspace forms like the Internet and the World Wide Web reconstitute the Habermasian public sphere, a venue for "free speech," or will they turn out to be as restricted as, say, current broadcast media?
. What does the decoupling of space from place suggest about knowledge production, generalization, and dissemination--about science and education?
. What does this shift suggest about the reframing nationality, ethnicity, gender, class, sexual orientation, and other dimensions of identity?
. Does the decoupling further or reverse "the eclipse of community?"

5. Issues if the Ethnography of Virtual Work

At a minimum, the questions identified in the previous section indicate that something rather important is at stake in the transition to cyberspace. In the time remaining, I wish to focus on what cyberethnography has to suggest about work in cyberspace, or virtual work. Let us define "work" cross-culturally and evolutionarily as those institutions through which humans/cyborgs provide their societies with and distribute those things used for individual and social reproduction. We can then generate a list of cyberspace developments in regard to work with potentially momentous implications:

5.1. Cyberwork as a Social Activity: Ubiquitous Computing

In an earlier era, the problem of how to design a usable computer was conceived in individualistic, psycholgistic (as well as sexist) terms, e.g., the "man/machine interface." As evidenced by the popularity of approaches like Computer-Supported Cooperative Work, Groups Support Systems, Joint Application Design and Participatory Design, computer professionals have apparently finally discovered what work ethnography knew all along: That work is a profoundly social activity. The design problem of cyberspace has thus become how to develop information systems that support work socially.

At Xerox Palo Alto Research Center, the answer is, "through ubiquitous computing." This is the partly a question of designing office environments with the equivalent of "a monitor in every sandbox": "live" white boards which, like an Apple Newton, automatically convert written script into digitized information, one of a wide range of Input/Output devices which allow rapid access everywhere. More important than the hardware, however, is the conceptual shift involved in making everyone equally responsible for the shared data bases to which they all have equal access. In particular, for such environments to work, information must be a truly shared resource, not something held by those with power.

5.2. Cyberorganizations as Virtual: Reinventing Government outside of Government

It is but a short step from making computing possible everywhere in an organization to seeing an organization as possible wherever there is computing. As Darrah's families make clear, contemporary organizations are increasingly decoupled from place. For at least some organizations, this also means their boundaries become socially permeable as well as geographically diffuse.

For example, Phil Endress, the Mental Health Commissioner with whom I work in Oneida County, New York, likes to describe his job as "reinventing government outside of government." Initially, this meant privatization; his office has gone from employing over 130 people, most of whom were involved in delivering mandated mental health services to indigent clients, to about six. Those who were privatized are delivering similar services to similar clients, but they are employed by twenty or so not-for-profit agencies on thirty-odd different contracts.

But only for the moment. The "end of welfare as we know it," managed care, and block granting together mean further changes. For example, the 15 Heath Maintenance and Behavioral Health Care Organizations interested in managing public funds under contract in Oneida County will not want to have to contract with each service agency, let alone each private service provider, as diagrammed on the first chart. "Networking" is the future for those organizations which are to survive when programs are no longer mandated but outcomes are. Similarly, without services to provide, or regulations to enforce, what happens to the County Mental Health Department? Does it disappear, or does it find the new kinds of role implied in the second chart:

- mediator between HMOs/BHCOs, on the one hand, and networks of providers on the other;
- facilitator of networking, through identifying and removing blocks to establishing relationships;
- promoter of information sharing, both about existing organizations and of data about populations served and unmet needs; and
- monitor of the public good, especially identifying "holes in the safety net."

My point is that such virtual organizations are increasingly likely to be the mode. This is not primarily because of technological artifacts but because of the TANs created by the coming together of new social policies, other social developments, and new artifacts. This ordering is meaningful; despite my best efforts to find them, I know of very few NFPs which use AIT to model, let alone create, these new virtual organization TANs. Instead, like most private and public organizations, they only use AIT for management information systems, not as general systems for directing organizational change and strategy.

5.3. Organizational "Chain of Command" as Oxymoron: Teams, Matrices, and Internal and External Networks

Organizational theorists are no longer the only ones to have less and less tolerance for the traditional hierarchical organization, in which information flowed up from the bottom, and control flowed down from the top. Instead, we get

- "Team" forms of organization, and more cooperative, role-permeable, basketball or soccer-like, rather than football-like, teams;
- Matrix organizations, where people take up multiple roles in different projects, based on their personal preferences, and there is no permanent responsibility structure;
- Internal networks, perhaps congeries of mini-hierarchies, teams, and matrixed projects, within the 'same" organization; or
- External networks, similar to internal ones except that they cross organizational as well as geographic boundaries.

In such situations, it becomes increasingly difficult to talk about "the organization" and the work" as we have in the past; both organizations and work practices become "virtual."

5.4. Engineering Culture: The Second Parallel, Cultural Labor Process

Precisely because in the virtual organization the "terms and conditions" of the job become more difficult to define, the actual social interactions at work become more important. My colleagues and I at the State University spend an increasing proportion of our time responding to ever-more bizarre initiatives to form badly-conceived "partnerships" and "strategic alliances," coupled with thinly veiled attacks on the very notion of accessible public higher education. I call this the Ivan Boesky/hostile takeover era in public higher ed. Increasingly, as at Kunda's Tech, the business of the contemporary organization, working through BPR, TQM, JAD, QWL, etc., is the production and manipulation of culture, the marketing of the organization itself, even to itself, rather than goods or services.

I believe the most important characteristic of our current organizational era is the rise of the second parallel labor process. The commodification of the labor process was first institutionalized in the late 18th Century, involving the creation of the first detailed division of labor in manufactories for large scale production. In the late 19th, century much production was further commodified by separating production from conception. Perceived to be necessary in order to use Taylorist scientific management and self-controlled machines, this separation necessitated instituting a parallel paper labor process staffed by a white collar army of engineers, managers, secretaries, clerks, messengers, filers, accountants, sales staff, etc. The parallel paper process ran along side the physical labor process of production and soon cost as much to run.

Today's workplace increasingly manifests a second parallel process. At Kunda's Tech, new workers take classes in "the culture" and "Tech talk," and all workers participate in and give public testimonials at the ritualistic speeches by managers which have much more the flavor of a high school pep rally than a business meeting, let alone an English annual organizational meeting or an old-style Norwegian *allmoete*.

To an anthropologist, these processes of
. making the culture in the workplace explicit and, more importantly,
. treating its performance as itself a source of value

are the developments most worth watching. You may be aware of the large business literature which tells us that the profitability correlates of advanced information technology (AIT) are highly variable. I submit to you that it is their contribution to the production of workplace culture which is the characteristic most predictive of AITs contribution to profitability. That the relationship of AIT to the rise of the cultural labor process is highly ideological is suggested by Ken Erickson's study of meatcutting in the US midwest (1995). Erickson documents a great deal of interest in and talk about computer-based machines for high tech animal disassembly, yet virtually none of these rhetorically featured artifacts are used much "on the shop floor." Instead, the major recent technological innovation has been to increase to three the number of protective layers worn by workers. This "armor" separates meat cutters' activities from their own and their colleagues bodies, while they continue to disassemble carcasses, hung from automated moving overhead chains, in more or less the same way they have since the 1880s.

Thus, while the actual process of cutting meat have changed little, what has changed is the social relations manifest in it: the virtual elimination of trade unions from the industry, elimination of most of the experienced workforce, a drastic cut in average wages, a substantial decline in substantive worker skill as well as length of employment-- which in the plant Erickson studied now averages about six months--, an increase in workplace accidents, and a shift to Third world workers. Accompanying these changes, which are similar industry-wide, is a phenomenal growth in time spent on safety training, QWL, and other "culture" committees. All these factors, including the last, are encountered so frequently that we are justified in seeing them as parts of a new workplace regime. In the brave new world of meat, the primary role of AIT, frequently evoked but rarely used, is ideological. The technological incantations performed here wrap a particular workplace intervention with the aura of general inevitability. As the technological "bridge to the future" decouples space from place, work is decentered from the material and recentered on the cultural.

5.5. The end of work? Deskilling? The fracturing of identity?

Several recent books--e.g., Rifkin's The End of Work, Aronowitz and deFazio's *The Jobless Future*, Stoll's *Silicon Snake Oil*--revive the compputropian discourses of the first period of CR speculation. In addition to arguing that AIT destroys jobs, they also echo Harry Braverman's "deskilling" hypothesis. In his 1974 book *Labor and Monopoly Capital: The Degradation of Work in the Twentieth Century*, Braverman identifies a long-term tendency toward decline in the level of skill required of the average worker. He explains this decline as a consequence of the kinds of technologies which managers tend to choose, technologies which have deskilling as a common characteristic. Braverman traces this tendency to class dynamics, arguing that skilled workers have more substantial collective, class power. Because unskilled workers have both less power at the point of production and in the community, they are therefore less able to pursue a class interest. Braverman argues specifically that the spread of computer-based typing pools in large organizations is a contemporary example of the same dynamic.

In the early 1980s, Adam Schaff raised an additional question about the impact of AIT on work, not just its disemploying or deskilling tendencies: What would be the social psychological consequences for a civilization in which individual identity is based on work of mass structural disemployment?

Rifkin and Aronowitz/deFazio build further but also transform parts of these analyses. In particular, they step back some from Braverman's emphasis on class dynamics, tending instead to see the technology itself as inherently deskilling and disemploying. My own view is that the data on the direct employment, skill, and social psychological correlates of AIT are very mixed and difficult to read. Further, cyberethnography on work suggests that situations like that described by Erickson are much more common than "straight" deskilling/disemploying. For example, while word processing in typing pools doubtlessly marginalized some secretaries, the subsequent spread of the PC meant that, in many organizations, the pools were disbanded and secretarial services re-decentralized back into offices. As compared to her 1960s counterpart, the 1990s secretary has doubtless lost some typing skills (e.g., accuracy of typing and spelling), but she has learned some new ones and still has a comparably broad range of duties. Similarly, in contemporary social service, many jobs are being lost. This cannot be because AIT is being substituted for them, because so little AIT is used. Rather, political decisions end programs and cut funds.

What has declined significantly is the ability of workers to exercise collective power over the labor process. This is because their ability to do so in the past was enhanced by a relatively stable Industrial Relations climate and supportive state and especially national legislation. As labor processes have changed, so have occupational structures, lessening the power of unions which have been tied to old labor markets. Similarly, nations have given up, or chosen not to try to reassert, their national powers over economy in relation to changing conditions. AIT developments have clearly driven some changes in work process and made some legislation more possible, but they have been implemented in TANs which themselves incorporate other social imperatives with equally strong causal roles.

In sum, our capacity to predict the social implications of further introduction of AIT cannot be based on study of the artifacts alone. Will trade unions find ways to adapt to the changes in labor processes? Similarly, the decoupling of space from place have robbed some potential collectivities of older potential points of mobilization, such as shared identities. Will communities, workers, nations, and consumers find new relations in cyberspace on which to foster networks which counter the increased power of corporations? These questions are just as important as technical ones in trying to envision the virtual workspace.

6. Virtual Libraries

6.1. Democratizing Information--Not Yet!

In his 1990 book, *Democratizing Information: On-line Databases and the Rise of End-User Searching*, cyber-anthropologist (and computer manual writer) Brain Pfaffenberger addresses several issues of particular interest to special librarians. One is the question implied in his title: Whether on-line access to bibliographic databases substantially broadened general access to information in society. His answer, a negative, ran contrary to a common computopian claim: that AIT would neutralize many of the geographic and disciplinary advantages of those living close to good libraries and with professional credentials.

Pfaffenberger's argument was that the particular indexing conventions built into on-line bibliographic data bases insure that few non-professional "end-users"--only the most frequent and most skilled--would be able to use them effectively on their own. Most users still require a search intermediary, such as a librarian, to execute searches which provide a manageable number of appropriate references.

The reason why the new technologies of information access do not result in a broadening of unmediated access is the particular way in which on-line indexing conventions have developed. These are essentially a compromise between the "brute force" indexing which is possible with computers and the indexing conventions long a part of librarians craft knowledge and practice. Pfaffenberger's book is mostly an account of the profoundly social way in which this compromise was constructed.

6.2. Liquidation of the Search Intermediary (Librarian)--Not Yet Either!

The long-term effect of this social construction, Pfaffenberger argues, is increased job security for those librarians who master the technology. This is because computerization hides from view the operation of professional indexing at the same time as it increases the power to produce good searches of those individuals who understand the conventions.

If Pfaffenberger is right, the substitution of CD-ROM searching for on-line services like Dialog shouldn't make all that much difference, especially for special librarians, since, as I understand it, your organizations place a high priority on really good searches. I'd like to know if this is your experience.

6.3. Commoditization and Other Threats to Information Access

In a 1982 article, sociologist Susan Esterbrook identified another AIT-based, compputropian threat to the library. As "information" became a more valued factor of production, its value as a commodity would rise. This commoditization would inevitably lead to restricted access, and especially public and academic libraries would find themselves marginalized from the best information.

Fifteen years later, it hasn't, yet and in general, worked out this way. Contemporary compputropians make similar points about the commoditization of the World Wide Web, the colonization of cyberspace by commercial enterprises, and the current concern with so-called "intellectual property rights." I say "so-called" not because there are no genuine issues regarding control of information in cyberspace--there are--but because "intellectual property rights are not at the heart of the issue given this label. At the heart *is* the problem of how to make money off the use of a distribution medium much of whose basic structure has been explicitly developed for the *free* distribution of information.

As someone who has been teaching the use of computers for twenty five years now, I am very concerned about problems of information access. I am more computopian than compputropian about the commoditization issue, at least for the moment. This is because of the tremendous investment in the development of WWW presences by commercial enterprises, basically because

1) they see Web sites (somewhat inappropriately) as fantastic advertising opportunities; and

2) when consumers order goods through Web sites producers can realize greater value by cutting out middlemen--e.g., stores, distributors, etc.

My hunch is that in the near future access to the web, if not the Web, will rival access to catalogue shopping and cable television, if not free broadcast television. If I am right, cyber-librarians main problems will turn out to be neither loss of jobs, skill, nor identity but:

6.4. Infoglut and Infogluttony

As a teacher, it often feels like my main difficulty is overcoming my students' well-developed defenses against information. Everyone in employment-based social formations must develop mechanisms to screen out most of the flood of information which washes over us from other people and our environment, let alone the more obvious billboards, broadcast media advertisements, leaflets, etc. If you are like me, you find a main impediment to getting anything done the inordinate amount of time you spend reading through email each day. Perhaps like me you avoid "surfing the Web" because you find it too easy to consume large blocks of time hopping from one interesting site to another.

Again, the answer to the increasing amount of electronically-distributed information, and to the gluttonous tendencies which follow for some of us, is not, by and large, technological. The kinds of programs one can build to help screen information are limited by the extent to which

. the user is capable of articulating her actual information interests,
. incoming messages are indexed in a way which fits this articulation, and
. the indexing is standardized.

I am, of course, reiterating Pfaffenberger's main point--that the kinds of information accessing skills at the heart of the librarians craft are more rather than less necessary in really existing cyberspace--in regard to a slightly different issue.

Cyberethnographers like me--indeed, all Cyberians, whether conscious colonizers or not--need good librarians even more. Indeed, I would argue that the rate of growth in the volume of information will rapidly make acute an already troubling problem for any intellectual. I mean the increasingly tenuous connection between, and the precipitously declining ratio of, information and/to knowledge. Among other things, this problem is a consequence of the confluence of the increasing penetration of the commodity form into cyberspace and the ways in which TANs like the World Wide Web makes personal publishing much easier.

The librarians I have known have generally tried to be neutral toward information, to act as if "all information is created equal" and place their professional emphasis more on helping users access it and less on evaluating its quality. While still noble in theory, I believe that infoglut makes this position increasingly untenable in practice. Special librarians in particular will be asked increasingly not only to help users articulate their standards for evaluating information but also to exercise those standards on behalf of their organization in general and specific users in particular. This is just one reason why librarians will inevitably be important as active constructors of, not just travelers in, cyberspace.

6.5. Appropriate Response to the Declining Academic Accessibility of Print

I do not wish to be interpreted as saying there are no reasons for concern regarding access to information. Librarians like Nancy Kranich have, in my view, provided an admirable "call to arms" by pointing out some of the possible consequences of recent telecommunications reform initiatives. Rather, to be dealt with effectively, these threats must be confronted in a detailed and specific manner, and that we can do this in part through professional activity.

To see what I have in mind, example, consider the difficult situation of librarians at academic institutions. On the one hand, the increasing number of CD-ROM based search aids mean students are increasingly aware of the intellectual materials potentially relevant to their study needs. The increasing proportion of acquisition budgets allocated to buying these aids, plus the increasing cost of books and paper journals, results in a paradox: *increasing* awareness of resources but *decreasing* actual access to them. More efficient inter-library loan can help, but this is unlikely to relieve the situation substantially. (I have been working with a colleague, Tom Hassler, on a computer object, a Gnobot, to help.)

Students are responding by increasingly surfing the Web for tools; I submit that this will happen much more in the future. Those intellectual practices with the earliest, best constructed, and most substantial presence on the Web will be in the best position to attract the attention of students as well as broader publics and therefore to have influence with them. Members of my professional organization, the American Anthropological Association, want to make the *American Anthropologist* the flagship of American anthropology, the site of intellectual practice to which people turn when they think of anthropology. Their prospects for accomplishing this are much better through a Web-based, cyberspace strategy than the Guttenburg strategy, a campaign to promote the *AA* as a print journal, outlined in the AAA long range plan.

For reasons like this, I am urging the AAA to commit itself to moving rapidly, as opposed to the current slowly and warily, into cyberspace. The strategy I envision will have several elements. One will be a serious professional home page, with links to AAA activities, academic and non-academic groups and departments, other anthropological and social/natural science activities, and individual anthropologists. Another will be free, electronic publication of eventually most if not all AAA publications. A third will be maintenance of and provision of access to multiple data bases, of members, of anthropologists in general, of anthropologists with relevant public expertise, of minority scholars, etc. A fourth will be maintenance of and support for listserves, electronic project groups, etc. A fifth would be a policy dimension, to plan strategically for anthropology's collective intervention in the cultural construction of cyberspace. A sixth would be CMC dimensions at the annual meetings--e.g., e-sessions in which papers were circulated electronically beforehand so that the session could involve much more substantive writer-audience interaction, less performance. A seventh would be promotion of ethnographic research on the cultural construction of cyberspace, research with direct, practical relevance to the implementation of the cyberspace strategy outlined here. An eighth would be active liaison with other academic/intellectual groups attempting to make a similar transition.

There are important practical problems with the strategy I propose. One is the problem of unequal access to cyberspace by anthropologists themselves, along dimensions like gender, race, and geography. Still, I increasingly find myself in meeting with anthropologists all of whom have email addresses. Moreover, through our university, N.G.O., and commercial connections, we should be able to provide access (e.g., through "guest" or "community" accounts) for all anthropologists, in a manner similar to providing library access for visiting scholars. Another dimension of access is actually reading the stuff; many of us are used to paper, like books and journals on our shelves, etc. I personally would like fewer scholarly publications, but more important is the need for a collective decision to use these new media, and to find ways to train ourselves to take advantage of what they have to offer, and to compensate for their admittedly serious drawbacks. The sooner we begin, the better we will become.

7. Conclusion: The Dialectics of Futurework: Decoupled from Place, Coupled More Tightly to Both Technology and Society

A second set of problems for the kind of program I wish the AAA to pursue are intimately library-related: maintaining adequate archives of electronic publications, insuring integrity of text, establishing standards for citing Web sites, etc. These are issues which anthropologist and scholars from other fields should be pursuing more vigorously with librarians.

From one point of view, such issues are problems. Yet all scholars share with librarians in cyberspace a related opportunity, to redefine some basic dimensions of scholarly activity. Can we, for example, use approaches like CSCW to lessen the individualism so encouraged by contemporary academic career paths, to share texts across space and time and generate more collective, mutable "products?"

In conclusion, I draw your attention to EP Thompson's pithy characterization of workers, in *The Making of the English Working Class* (1963): As being a significant presence at their own social birth. Like the Chartists, Luddites, and Republicans to which Thompson draws attention, late Twentieth Century scholars can only chose to be more or less reluctant co-creators of cyberspace; we are by our being compelled to be colonizers. Special librarians, like other intellectuals, can also chose to create together or separately, but I believe that you must choose to be active creators of cyberspace, if you are to continue to do an effective job of providing information to your organizations as they transition to the brave new virtual workspace.

8. References

Anderson, B.
    1983. *Imagined communities: Reflections on the origin and spread of nationalism*. London: Verso.
Darrah, C.
    1995. "Techno-Guanxi: Connecting relationships and icons through technology." [Paper Presented at the Annual Meeting, American Anthropological Association]. Washington, DC.
Dennett, D.
    1991. *Consciousness explained*. Boston: Little, Brown.
Erickson, K. C.

1995. "Reskilling the Jungle: Multilinugal Craft Knowledge in a High Plains Boxed-Beef Factory." [Paper Presented at Annual Meeting, American Anthropological Association]. Washington, DC.

Esterbrook, S.
1984. "Commoditizing library information." In *My troubles are going to have trouble with me.* Sacks, Karen, and Dorothy Remy, eds. New Brunswick, NJ: Rutgers University Press.

Gibson, W.
1984. *Neuromancer.* New York.

Hakken, D.
forthcoming. *Cyborgs@cyberspace: The ethnography of the future?* New York: Routledge.
1993. "Computing and social change: New technology and workplace transformation, 1980-1990." *Annual Review of Anthropology,* 22, 107-2. Palo Alto: Annual Reviews.
---------, with Barbara Andrews
1993. *Computing myths, class realities: An ethnography of technology and working people in Sheffield, England.* Boulder, CO: Westview Press.

Hannerz, U.
1992. *Cultural complexity: Studies in the social organization of meaning.* New York: Columbia University Press.

Kunda, G.
1992. *Engineering culture: Control and commitment in a high-tech corporation.* Philadelphia: Temple University Press.

Pfaffenberger, B.
1990. *Democratizing Information: Online Data-bases and the Rise of End-User Searching.* Boston: G.K. Hall.

Rifkin, J.
1995. *The end of work: The decline of the global labor force and the dawn of the post-market era.* New York: G.P. Putnam's Sons.

Schaff, A.
1982. "Occupation vs. work." In *Microelectronics and society: A report to the club of Rome* (G. Friedrichs, and Adam Schaff, Eds) (pp. 322-333). New York: New American Library.

Thompson, E. P.
1963. *The making of the English working class.* New York: Random House.

Wallace, A. F. C.
1970. *Culture and personality* (2nd ed.). New York: Random House.

Williams, R.
1989. *Resources of hope: Culture, democracy, socialism.* London: Verso.

Freedom, Accountability, and Community: An Approach to Designing Alternative Workplaces

**Presentation to the Special Libraries Association State-of-the-Art-Institute
"The Virtual Workplace: One Size Doesn't Fit All"**

Eric Richert, Sun Microsystems, Inc.
November, 1996

Freedom, Accountability, and Community:
An Approach to Designing Alternative Workplaces.
Presentation to the Special Libraries Association State of the Art Institute
"The Virtual Workplace: One Size Doesn't Fit All"
November, 1996

Introduction

Sun Microsystems, Inc. and other ground-breaking companies in the information and communications technology industry are driving change in the way people and companies conduct business and do their work. Interestingly, while Sun and others are rapidly developing (and are fluent in) the technologies that are enabling this change, they are themselves struggling with the *impacts* of these changes on their own workforces, work processes, work organizations, and work settings, and with how best to turn these impacts to competitive advantage.

A common approach to converting these impacts to advantage is through the cost savings that technology can generate, whether through automation, re-engineering, or through reductions in other resources such as people and real estate. Another approach, much discussed but little understood,[1] is improving the revenue-generating capabilities of the workforce. While Sun is certainly investigating and implementing cost savings through the use of its own technology products, it is also seriously exploring the revenue side of the equation, and the role of the workplace in this productivity effort. This presentation reviews that exploration.

To begin, I will briefly review the transformation of work that is driving the need to consider new work environments. I will end with the conclusion that one size indeed does not fit all.

Transformation of Work

The largest groups of workers at the beginning of the 20th century can roughly be placed into four categories: farmers; domestic servants; professionals or craftsmen who worked as sole-proprietors or in small groups (doctors, wood-workers, merchants, teachers, and the like); and workers in large manufacturing organizations executing the decisions of others, largely through manual labor. The managers of that labor comprised a relatively small group.

The work of these large organizations was to process raw materials into finished physical goods. Their labor force was of limited literacy and "required no skills they did not already possess"[2] as farmers or domestic servants, nor any additional knowledge.

---

[1] For example, much has been written about the "productivity paradox" which refers to the large annual investments made in information technology with no apparent productivity increases at the group or aggregate level.
[2] Peter Drucker, "A Century of Social Transformation," Managing in a Time of Great Change (Truman Talley books, New York City, 1995), p.224

In the large organizations that employed this labor force, "the major problem of organization was efficiency in the performance of the manual worker who did what he had been told to do."[3] This challenge gave rise in the early 20th century to Frederick Taylor's principles of "scientific management," including the following: 1) Managers should reduce necessary knowledge to rules, laws, and formulae; 2) All possible brain work should be removed from the shop and centered in a planning department; and 3) The work of each worker should be fully planned with each worker receiving detailed instructions for the task at hand, as well as for the means to accomplish that task.[4]
As the 20th century progressed, the numbers of farmers and domestic servants declined, and the population of blue collar, or industrial, workers rose dramatically. "In the 1950's, industrial blue collar workers had become the largest single group in every developed country."[5] Mostly their work was designed and managed to fit the scientific management paradigm.

This paradigm of work was not limited to the manual labor of factories. It also applied to much of the expanding "white collar" population that processed flows of paper (as in the banking and insurance industries and in expanding governmental agencies).

Important underlying assumptions of this work paradigm included these: 1) The vast majority of workers did not need to make decisions of any significance; 2) Therefore, they did not need to have a view of the intent or strategies of the enterprise, nor an understanding of the work of the enterprise beyond the scope (and rules) of their specific jobs; 3) All work came to the worker in predictable ways, to a single location, for predictable processing; and 4) The single location was centralized to enhance the control and "monitoring of the production process, use of materials" and general quality of work and work output.[6] In addition, prior to the second half of the 20th century, neither information nor transportation technology was available to support or promote work activities that extended much beyond a local or regional area.

By 1959 this paradigm was changing sufficiently for Peter Drucker to coin the term "knowledge worker." He did so to identify a newly emerging group of workers who "use knowledge, theory, and concept rather than physical force or manual labor."[7] These were and are technologists of many types (lab and paramedical, for example), R&D engineers and scientists, market researchers, product planners, manufacturing system designers, advertisers and purchasers, service and support personnel in direct contact with customers, and so on.[8] This group, according to Drucker, had become by the 1990's the

---

[3] Peter Drucker, The Effective Executive (Harper Collins, New York City, 1966) p. 2
[4] Jeffrey Pfeffer, Competitive Advantage Through People (Harvard Business School Press, Boston, 1994) p. 126
[5] Peter Drucker, "A Century of Social Transformation," p. 221
[6] Jeffrey Pfeffer, p.122
[7] Peter Drucker, The Effective Executive, p. 3
[8] Peter Drucker, "A Century of Social Transformation," p.237

predominant work group in the United States, and now comprises a larger percentage of the workforce than blue collar workers ever did.

Some of these knowledge workers continue to perform routine jobs. Most, however, are and will be called upon to make choices and decisions on behalf of the organization in the normal course of their work--this makes their work by definition non-routine--and will be held accountable for those decisions. They will be "responsible for a contribution that materially affects the capacity of the organization to perform and to obtain results."[9] That contribution will be based on the *effectiveness* or *rightness* of their choices and decisions, not on the efficiency with which the decisions are made. Importantly, these decision-making workers do and will span the organizational ranks, from highest executive to individual contributors, in order to exploit a necessarily wide range of specialized knowledge and enable broad knowledge creation. Even certain blue collar jobs have been imbued with specialized technology to the extent that they fit the decision-making work characteristics of the new paradigm.[10]

The forces that have brought about this shift in the nature of work are many and complex. Drucker suggests that the GI Bill in the United States after World War II caused a four-year college education to become as common as a high school education prior to the war, driving a high level of expectation of a shift in the nature of work.[11] Robert Johansen suggests that the Vietnam War changed the metaphor of work from one of "a machine...that could be fine-tuned like an automobile engine" to one that recognizes that human beings who make up an enterprise "blend their collective wills [to create] complex yet flexible webs of interconnection."[12] Further, according to Johansen, "the oil shocks of the seventies sent American industry reeling", causing much discussion and acknowledgment of the new complexities of America's competitive environment; and that the Challenger tragedy in 1986 "revealed serious flaws in the management structure of large projects." Certainly, advances in information and transportation technologies have both fed the shift in the nature of work, and been a product of that shift as well.

Whatever the forces, the results are clear. Business today involves global markets, global competition, and global workforces; projects too complex for any individual or isolated group of individuals to grasp and execute independently, whether the project is product development, a marketing campaign, or a sale to a large customer; and a business environment too large, too fast moving, and too complex for small groups of executives alone to track and provide strategic response. The notion of strategic planning

---

[9] Peter Drucker, The Effective Executive, p. 5

[10] "The New Factory Worker", Business Week, September 30, 1996

[11] Peter Drucker, "A Century of Social Transformation," p. 229

[12] Robert Johansen and Rob Swigert, Upsizing the Individual in the Downsized Organization (Addison-Wesley, Reading, MA, 1994) pp. 4-16

departments, so much a part of scientific management, has been discredited, with a new call for "business unit managers [to] take full and effective charge of the strategy-making process" and further for that process to be "emergent", that is, rising out of action rather than out of analytic planning.[13]

These results mean that for an organization to perform well, people need to be viewed not as standardized (and thus interchangeable) components in a pre-planned production process, but rather as a vital source of diversity to understand the constantly changing external environment; to articulate organizational intent; to develop new strategies and knowledge aligned with that intent; to distribute and use that knowledge in the production of new products and services; and to understand the impact of these innovations on the external environment and, thus, on the organization itself.

The many people who need to be involved with this work will probably not be co-located, or even co-employed.[14] Certainly, the work of many will not generally be delivered to a single location for processing. Instead, employees will work across time and distance (whether "down the hall" or across continents) to connect with fellow employees, partners, vendors, and customers in order to create, distribute, and use the knowledge necessary for successful organizational performance. The unpredictability of organizational intent, of the locations for work, and of when and with whom work will need to be accomplished, are all hallmarks of the new work paradigm called knowledge work.

Freedom, Accountability, and Community

Knowledge work is the work by which most of today's businesses achieve intent.

Business intent is vision or strategy that creates a gap between an organization's current and needed capabilities. Gaps that are small will tend to generate incremental change. Gaps that are large will drive (albeit with substantial risk) more revolutionary change. Business intent can be visionary in nature, or more specifically related to a new market, customer, product, or process goal. Whatever the nature of business intent, the gap it creates is filled by the organization through the type of knowledge work that we define as innovation: the creation and exploitation of new ideas.[15]

---

[13] Henry Mintzberg, "The Fall and Rise of Strategic Planning", Harvard Business Review, Jan-Feb 1994, pp107-112

[14] Charles Handy, The Age of Unreason (Harvard Business School Press, Boston, 1989) p.31

[15] Rosabeth Moss Kanter, "When A Thousand Flowers Bloom", Research in Organizational Behavior edited by Barry M. Staw and L.L. Cummings, Vol. 10, pp. 169-211, 1988.

The creation and exploitation of new ideas require conditions very different from those required to accomplish work envisioned by scientific management. Three necessary conditions are: 1) Freedom to act; 2) Accountability for actions; and 3) Participation in community. These conditions are strongly linked: knowledge work begins with individual insight which, when aligned with intent, becomes useful to the organization through the social process of combining with the insights of others. No one condition can be successfully satisfied in the absence of either of the other conditions.

Freedom to Act

Freedom of individuals and of groups of individuals to act enables an enterprise to generate and combine a large number of ideas based on: wide ranging information gathering and sharing; many individuals' unique experiences, perspectives, and specialized knowledge; and informal and formal dialogue that creates a common understanding of and commitment to business intent. Freedom to act also enables an enterprise to exploit more quickly and effectively those ideas which are accepted as most likely to achieve business intent.

Essentially, freedom to act is the ability of an individual, team, or group to make choices and decisions and then to *act* on those decisions. Freedom to act includes the ability to decide when, where, how, and with whom to accomplish the work at hand. Importantly, this freedom includes crossing organizational and functional boundaries within a company, between company and customer, and between company and competitors when this is appropriate.

This freedom is predicated on: 1) An understanding of and commitment to the intent of the organization (its overarching goals, its strategies for achieving those goals, and specific business initiatives related to those goals); 2) Access to the information necessary to develop legitimate decision alternatives; 3) An understanding of and respect for the roles and responsibilities of others associated with the same business challenge; 4) An ability to reach across organizational and company boundaries to secure necessary ideas, knowledge, and skills; and 5) Acceptance of accountability for results of decisions made and actions taken.

Accountability for Actions

Freedom to act is balanced and indeed enabled by accountability: personal acceptance of responsibility for actions and results; commitment to the intent of the organization; willingness to sort through roles and responsibilities among a project group, since these may well change from project to project; commitment to sharing personal and organizational knowledge and lessons learned, and using that knowledge appropriately; and energy and effort to maintain linkages with and within the organization even when time and distance make this difficult.

Without these commitments, efforts, and accountabilities, freedom to act yields confusion and chaos, and is likely to be reined in and/or replaced by bureaucratic procedures to re-establish order. Accountability, rather than the rules, laws, and formulae of scientific management, helps provide the necessary alignment within a large and diverse workforce striving to achieve business intent.

Participation in Community

The creation and exploitation of ideas is fundamental to an organization's ability to achieve intent. While creation of ideas—development of insight—is often the domain of individuals[16], the exploitation of those ideas—evolving the ideas into new knowledge that is distributed and used in the organization—is a social, or community, activity:

> "Organizational knowledge creation should be understood as a process that 'organizationally' amplifies the knowledge created by individuals and crystallizes it as a part of the knowledge network of the organization. This process takes place within an expanding 'community of interaction', which crosses...organizational levels and boundaries."[17]

Rosabeth Moss Kanter[18] and J.B. Quinn[19] also claim that innovation and knowledge creation are social activities: "The innovation process is knowledge-intensive...relying on individual human intelligence and creativity and involving 'interactive learning'." Susan Stucky of the Institute for Research on Learning (IRL) writes: "...social participation is central to human cognition. [We need to] support emergent social interactions for it is through those that organizational learning happens."[20] Stucky and her colleagues at IRL describe, for example, *communities of practice* through which new knowledge is created.

Freedom to act and participation in community can be thought of as contradictory conditions, but they are not. They are synergistic. Their synergy is achieved through rich and complex patterns of individual work (developing commitment and insight, and executing specific tasks) and social activity (sharing insight, combining insights into new knowledge, distributing and using that knowledge).

---

[16] Ikujiro Nonaka and Hirotaka Takeuchi, The Knowledge-Creating Company (Oxford University Press, New York City, 1995), p.225

[17] Nonaka and Takeuchi, p. 59

[18] Rosabeth Moss Kanter, p. 171

[19] J.B. Quinn, "Technological Innovation, Entrepreneurship and Strategy", Sloan Management Review, Spring 1979, pp. 19-30

[20] Susan U. Stucky, Technology in Support of Organizational Learning, p.2

However, these rich patterns of freedom and participation can be difficult to achieve, particularly when necessary linkages must span distance and time. This is the fundamental challenge of implementing what has become known as "alternative work environments," particularly the "virtual workplace," which typically implies a highly decentralized work environment, both organizationally and physically.

Alternative Work Environments

Language is an important indicator of a society's sense of what is real and "right". It is interesting to note that discussion of work environments that differ from the general paradigm of the industrial era still requires the adjective "alternative"! While the nature of work has changed profoundly, much of the environment that supports work has not.

We think of *alternative* work environments as integrated systems of resources that support knowledge work, through which businesses effectively create and achieve intent. The resources are organizational practice, technology, and physical architecture. Combined as systems, these resources support knowledge work by enabling (or appropriately inhibiting) the necessary conditions of freedom, accountability, and community.

It should be understood that the balance required between freedom, accountability, and community is dependent upon business intent and context. All three conditions are required, but in different degrees for different situations. This is why "one size" indeed "does not fit all."

A useful way to think of these conditions is to use Robert Keidel's terminology in describing human relationships, or behaviors and practices, as autonomous, controlling, or cooperative,[21] which map to freedom, accountability, and community respectively. This is useful for two reasons. First, these relationships are expressions of degrees and types of *linkages* between people. This is important because "the organizations producing innovation have more complex structures that *link* people in multiple ways to encourage them to 'do what needs to be done' (emphasis added)...."[22] Second, we can conceive of organizational, technological, and physical design features that might enable or inhibit these relationships. These are the features that comprise the work environment, which we can design to support the practices believed to be important for achieving business intent. The following table illustrates a few of these features, along with design choices that support the desired relationship:

---

[21] Robert W. Keidel, Seeing Organizational Patterns (Berrett-Kohler Publishers, San Francisco, 1995) p.6
[22] Kanter, p.172

Relationships

Feature	Autonomous	Controlling	Cooperative
Physical Architecture			
Work Setting	Decentralized	Centralized	Centralized
Workplace Type	Private/Individual	Status-Based	Group/Open
Work Space Layout	Dispersed	Linear	Clustered
Technology			
Technology Access	Remote	Central	Central/Remote
Technology Support	Anytime	Office Hours	Anytime
Technology Type	Nomadic	Fixed-in-Place	Networked
Organizational Practice			
Communication Mode	Asynchronous	Synchronous	Synchronous
Information Flow	Pooled	Sequential	Reciprocal
Organization Structure	Flat/Clear	Steep/Clear	Flat/Amorphous
Knowledge Transfer	Formal	Formal	Informal
Reward System	Individual	Hierarchic	Team
Management By	Results	Process	Results
Group Work	-	Planned	Spontaneous
Decision Making	Empowered	Directive	Consensus

A challenge in designing an alternative work environment is in coming to understand the relative importance of autonomous, controlling, and cooperative relationships. The design effort should not be one of maximizing all three types of relationships; rather one of optimizing through "emphasizing one or two variables without neglecting any."[23] The design effort must be grounded in a clear articulation of business intent, and in the practices or behaviors (relationships) that the business itself believes are critical to achieving that intent. Judgments can then be made about which features and which feature choices, *in concert with each other*, will most likely enable those behaviors.

A Framework for Making Work Environment Choices

At Sun, we have come to understand that a *very* wide range of choices exists for creating work environments, and that we need a framework, or model, first for guiding discussion and illuminating possibilities, and second for making feature choices that make sense given an understanding of business intent and important practices for achieving intent. Importantly, we also need a framework for evaluating whether the choices we make are successful after they have been implemented. We call the framework we have created our "Strategic Choice Framework," and it is through this framework that we explicitly make work environment choices that can range from the "traditional" to the "alternative" to the "virtual".

---

[23] Keidel pg. 24. This optimization is analogous to the necessary optimization of freedom, accountability, and community.

Framework Description[24]

Our framework is directional. Its output says: If business intent is to pioneer sales in new Latin American markets, and the relationships (behaviors, practices)[25] the business has identified as key to the success of this effort are…

- Spend as much time as possible with and responding to customers to build new, long-lasting relationships;
- Be opportunistic in the new geography, acting quickly to capture new sales and customers while using limited resources efficiently;
- Deliver focused, well prepared , up-to-date product and service information (pricing, options, configurations) consistent with the company's products-offered strategy and sales plan; and
- Rapidly share successes and failures with colleagues for dissemination of "what works and what does not" in this new market

…which we can categorize as autonomous, controlling, or cooperative (this exercise assures that all three of these types of relationships are addressed, but ranked in priority):

Autonomous	Controlling	Cooperative
Maximize Customer Face Time	Well Informed, Prepared	Collaborate in Sales Planning
Responsive to Customer	Deliver Consistent Message	Share Info with Colleagues
Work Anywhere/Anytime	Orchestrate Resources	
Access Information on Demand		
Opportunistic		
Understand Customer		

…then the following accommodations are necessary to support a high percentage of these critical practices:

- Provide the ability to be near and with the customer frequently
- Provide the ability to give the customer valuable product information rapidly and accurately
- Provide the ability for colleagues and partners to reach each other anytime, anywhere
- Provide time and place for planning and coordination activities
- Provide the ability to share information and lessons learned
- Provide economy of resources

---

[24] Iometrics, Inc., of Irvine, CA, has been instrumental in helping us develop this framework.

[25] In the context of our Famework, we call these relationships, practices, or behaviors "key success factors".

...and these accommodations can be translated into an array of enabling work environment features. The features chosen not only respond to the practices expressed as important to achieving success, they also reinforce each other in doing so:

Workspace Features	Technology Features	Org'l Practice Features
Office(s) Near Key Customers	Remote Technology Access	Management by Results
Unassigned Work Areas	Universal Log-in Connect	Formal Knowledge Mgmt
Quiet Individual Spaces	24 Hour Support	Planned Group Work
Fewer Offices than People	"Follow Me" Telephone	Empowered Decision Making
Group Spaces Available	Customer-focused Applic'ns	Manager as Integrator

This array of feature choices creates a "scenario" that directs the work environment designer towards a solution that might be termed a "drop-in center plus telework." The designer must then address a host of specific design challenges, but with confidence that the direction is likely to support the work that needs to be done to achieve the stated intent, and with confidence that the business and employees will be committed to that direction since they themselves have defined business intent and the needed relationships and practices.

Specifically, our framework requires: 1) Clear articulation of **business intent**, or desired business outcomes. This is "what" the business is trying to achieve. 2) Identification of the **key behaviors**, or work practices, needed to accomplish the desired business outcomes. This is "how" intent is to be achieved. These behaviors, individually and in the aggregate, will display a bias towards autonomy, control, or cooperation, or a combination of two of these without neglecting the third. 3) Identification of the physical, technological, and organizational practice **features,** and the specific feature characteristics, that can support the needed behaviors. 4) Development of work environment **scenarios** consisting of combinations of complementary physical, technological, and organizational practice features. Each scenario is a *system* of features that creates a work environment choice. 5) Assessment, using numeric ranges such as "from 0-100", of the relative importance or impact of features on behaviors, and of behaviors on outcomes. Expressing these judgments numerically helps make assumptions explicit; allows hypotheses to be made that predict **linkages** between features, behaviors and outcomes; and allows the framework to rank possible scenarios by the extent to which they satisfy key practices and business intent. 6) Creation of **metrics** that express the extent to which business intent is achieved, and the extent to which needed behaviors are employed, once the work environment system is in place.

The following diagram illustrates these framework components:

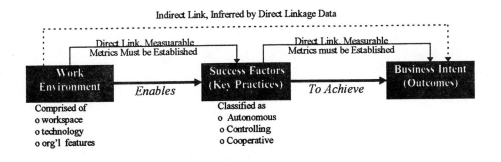

Framework Use

It is important to note again that use of this choice framework requires the committed participation by the business organization that will be affected by the choices made (the choice framework is not the domain of a scientific management style planning department!). The business organization must be the source of clear articulation of business intent, and of identification and ranking of the work practices that are key to achieving that intent. Designers of the work environment—a cross functional team of architectural, organizational, and technological experts—provide the expertise to propose the work environment features--integrated and matched to the key work practices--and then flesh out the feature specifications and design them as appropriate for the specific circumstance.

Conclusion

Workplaces different from the industrial era norm are often thought of as "virtual workplaces", driven by new technology and the need to lower costs associated with real estate. In fact, the virtual workplace is only one of many choices of workplace, technology is only one enabler of different kinds of work arrangements, and lower costs are only one of a number of possible outcomes.

Work environments consisting of organizational, technological, and physical features should be thought of as enablers of important work practices through which businesses can achieve specific strategies and goals. Many of today's work practices must be fashioned around the need to continuously create new organizational knowledge. Freedom to act, accountability for actions, and participation in community are three necessary conditions for these knowledge-creating work practices. However, the relative emphasis of each of these conditions, and related work practices, will vary according to the specific business situation. This is why one type of work environment, such as the virtual workplace, indeed does not fit all business needs.

Delivering Intelligence in the Virtual Ad Agency

Velda I. Ruddock, Director of Intelligence
TBWA Chiat/Day Advertising

for the
Special Libraries Association's State-of-the-Art Institute: The Virtual Workplace
Washington, DC, November 7-8, 1996

INTRODUCTION
Hello everyone. I'm really pleased to be here.

I want to talk about two things today: How our office changed the way we worked and the role of the Intelligence Department at TBWA Chiat Day.

I'll tell you about how in 1993 and 1994 we introduced the Team Architecture and Virtual Office concepts to our agency, knowing we needed to change the way we work to be successful. I'll tell you about some of our key lessons and I'll compare and contrast our primary offices — New York and Los Angeles. I'll also describe some of the changes our agency has experienced in the past three years and how these are affecting us.

The Intelligence Department has been integral in the process of how our agency has changed and I can't talk about one without the other. However, I will also tell you about our role, process and philosophy today.

I hope that when you leave you will be able to take away some of our lessons and ideas, whether you are already working in a virtual environment, thinking about it, or looking for a way to defend against it.

Who we are
Most of you will not be familiar with the name TBWA Chiat/Day. But you will recognize our work. We do the advertising and marketing for clients such as Nissan, Infiniti, Jack in the Box, America Online, Airtouch, Absolut Vodka, Sony Playstation, Wonderbra, and that pink bunny that keeps going... and going...

These are only some of our U.S. clients. We have offices on five continents.

Our advertising work is often considered provocative, edgy, challenging. It is a reflection of our attitude, our corporate culture. Some of our corporate rallying cries have included...

"Good enough is not enough"

"Innovate or die... and death is not an option."

"It's more fun to be the pirates than the navy"

and

"Chiat/Day and Night... if you don't come in
Saturday don't bother to come in Sunday"

It is exactly this kind of ballsy culture that made
changing the way we work possible.

HOW IT STARTED

In 1993, under the direction of our leader, the
visionary Jay Chiat, we started to look at what the
business world of the future would look like. We
saw massive and rapid change and we knew we
would need to change as well to survive, let alone
excel.

So we looked at how our people worked and found
definite flaws.

Although the agency had long ago jettisoned individual offices, we weren't using our resources as
efficiently as we might. Our dedicated desks, telephones and computers stood empty and unused
when employees were in meetings, at clients, or
working elsewhere. Our best work was not necessarily done at the office... or even during office
hours.

Also, like many offices, we lacked the necessary
tools, technology and for that matter, the necessary
mindset to work effectively.

Our file drawers were cluttered with old, misfiled,
and unknown material. Many documents were
duplicated throughout the agency taking up valuable space. Our computers were not networked and
contained files no one else had access to. Or just as
bad, people would store their files on disks and
when they left their intelligence left with them.

It wasn't the best way to work. We realized we did-
n't just need to reengineer our company; we needed
to undergo a major revolution.

— We needed to prepare ourselves to thrive regardless of what the future held.
— To be able to "morph" on command.
— We needed to leverage all of our resources and
  not be bound by personal and place or time-dri-
  ven constraints.

In other words, we needed to be strategic,
creative and flexible.

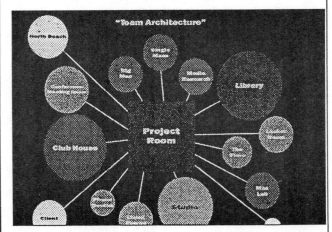

Team Architecture

What emerged was an organizational philosophy
that many have called the "virtual corporation"
because we committed to providing the tools and
the flexibility to allow our employees to work anywhere at any time.

We called what we did "Team Architecture" because
the team is central to the model and because the
concept was dedicated to collaborative workspace

and collective intelligence. At the time we didn't realize that these are two quite different models.

Our goal was to be as paperless and unburdened by unnecessary stuff as feasible. This required that employees "let go of" their space and their material possessions. In return we promised them the tools and freedom to work where and when it would be most effective. We also told them we would give them access to more information than they had.

This is what we did...

IMPLEMENTATION

Offsite Records Management
Offsite Records Management was the most dramatic way our entire office realized their life was going to change. It forced the first stages of mindset change.

Boxes prepared for Offsite Records Management

At our office offsite records management is not the black hole of storage many offices rent. For us it is an extension of the office and a part of our collective intelligence.

Information Resources establish the organizational procedures employees had to follow to catalog their materials in such a way that they can be retrieved whenever needed. And between September and December of 1993 Chiat/Day staff had the daunting task of purging their files and bookshelves, cataloging those items that needed to be kept.

This was hard. As we all know, information is power, and no one wanted to release their power. Asking people to catalog was a misery. Most people don't have a "cataloging" mind, and no one had much time to catalog. Just because we were going to change the way we worked didn't stop the regular workload. It was an ugly time of adjustment as each person went through the stages of loss: denial, rage, bargaining and finally acceptance.

Today we have an offsite records manager whom we fondly call the "Guardian Angel" (our offsite records management facility is called Guardian Records Management). Each day we have at least two organized "runs" and there often is an additional "managed rush." Hundreds of files, boxes and objects are moved back and forth each month.

Employees still don't like to catalog their materials. But they have discovered benefits. Not only can they retrieve their own "stuff," they often have access to files from other employees, if they clear the access requirements.

The work space
In one week, between Christmas and New Year we physically changed the interior of a whole building.

Employees were given the week between the two holidays off and when they came back there was very little designated desk space. I've heard that by going virtual we deleted a third of our work space in the LA office. It may have been more.

We believe that work can be done anywhere, at any time and with whomever you need. Personal cubicles didn't provide the added value collaborative space had, and we replaced them with project rooms, and other places employees could work in small groups or individually.

The project rooms are central to team collaboration and their ever changing walls document the thinking of the group.

But where they could work was not restricted to one time or place. Other areas included: work wells and small office areas, living rooms, small meeting areas, and a giant clubhouse. Personal items were kept in lockers.

Project room

Lockers

Living room

Tilt-A-Whirls

Intelligence Center

In the LA office we also built a large new central library called the Intelligence Center. The agency itself has several areas devoted to special collections and research, including a media research lab and a creative library. The Intelligence Center however is the place we offer collaborative resources for the entire agency.

The TBWA Chiat/Day Intelligence Center is a spacious wing equipped with 16 stationary Macintosh, an optical scanner and two CD-ROM workstations. There is also an enormous work table that seats 14 comfortably. The entire office, including this work table is wired for Macintosh computers.

There is a file room for current studies, picture files, concept files, vendor files, etc., and a separate periodicals room.

In our business, information dates quickly and there are very few periodicals we keep for more that a year. Yes, most of them are either online, on the internet or on CD-ROM, and we talked about not having them at all, but don't forget we're an ad agency and we need to see the ads in their natural habitat.

Intelligence Center

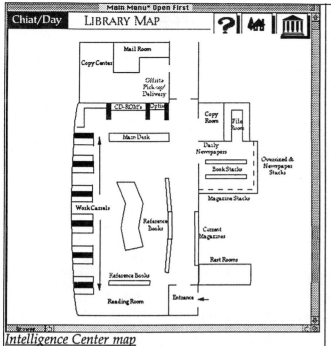
Intelligence Center map

The references and circulating collection are in the main room, as was a browsing magazine rack. There was also a comfortable reading room, complete with couches, easy chairs and ottomans. That room is also wired for computer access. The intelligence center is usually packed.

Technology

When we first went "virtual," we had no rule books. We made a best guess that for many employees a rule of thirds would likely apply: they would spend a third of their time in the office; a third of their time at their home office; and a third of their time in meetings and at other offsite work locations. It didn't matter where they worked because technology would provide the communication bridge.

What did this mean?

The agency vastly upgraded their computer system with hardware, software and connectivity. A powerful network provides employees with easy access to their files regardless of where they may be logged in.

The file servers are a reflection of how we organized our physical environment. The intention was that we make it possible for teams to share resources and responsibilities. For example, just as there are physical project rooms there are "virtual project rooms." Just as we have physical departments we also have "virtual departments" on the file server. We even have "virtual lockers" on the server. These personal folders are for confidential items like staff evaluations, personal correspondence, ... and in some cases, resumes.

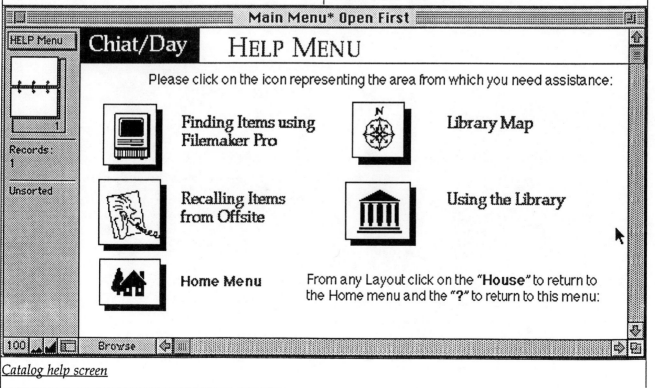
Catalog help screen

Central Intelligence

One of the virtual departments is Central Intelligence. It will come to no surprise to you that this is the electronic department folder administered by Information Resources. Here is where employees get their basic agency information, where they have access to a growing collection of internally produced reports and the agency's catalogs and databases. It is also where we have tips on how to use the technology, client logos, and public domain clip art.

Also on Central Intelligence were the catalog databases for offsite records management, the library and the magazine collection. We've tried to make the catalog databases easy to use with "point and click" buttons and help screens.

Applications

Obviously we updated all of our software as well as our hardware. I don't want to go through all of our applications but there are a couple you may be interested in.

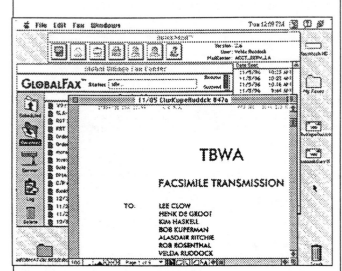

Fax document on virtual desktop

All our faxes are delivered to us through e-mail. We can open them up on our virtual desktop and save them for as long as we need, which is actually longer than our MIS staff would like. We love this application because it means we are not tied to a fax machine that is physically in one place. Regardless of where we are our faxes will be forwarded to us.

Almost all the major online and commercial services are available at the agency.

The pricy ones are only accessible through an Intelligence Officer and only with a job number. However, the commercial services like CompuServe, America Online, and Prodigy are available to everyone in the agency. We also provide four powerful end-user online databases on the Internet through a service called InSite and expect to subscribe to additional services.

All of the agency computers have Netscape as an application. Like many of you we have a world wide web site on the Internet (http://www.tbwachiatday.com). Also like many of you, we are developing an Intranet site. The Intelligence Department is a contributor to the external site, and responsible for much of the content inside the firewall.

www.tbwachiatday.com

At one time we had an inhouse public relations firm and we subscribed to a filtered news service. The service would alert us automatically through our e-mail every time a newswire with specific keywords was released. Although this waterfall news service is mandatory for PR folks for crisis prevention, it was overkill for the rest of us. We found that the sheer volume of e-mail placed an unnecessary burden on our servers and most people soon delegated the task of the waterfall to an assistant or asked to be taken off the list.

Scanning

When we first set out to design the virtual office we thought that any material not created on our file servers would be scanned. The goal was to be as paperless as we could be.

I'd like to say we've been successful ar this but we haven't been. Our New York office has come closer to that goal than we have and that is mostly because of the culture and the space prohibits saving paper. But I'll talk more about that later.

Optical imaging is not merely running documents through a scanner. There is a database function attached and careful indexing is mandatory or the documents will not be retrievable. Also, should you think scanning hardware and database software costs somewhere in the neighborhood of a fax machine, think again. Our system cost in the neighborhood of six figures.

Today we scan accounting records, electronic job jackets, materials we get from our clients and some of our vendor files. As you might expect, some groups wanted us to scan books and articles. This is clearly against the law and I won't put the agency at risk. Even with a membership to the Copyright Clearance Center this is not a good idea.

Issues

There were some computer- issues we needed to consider when we made our leap in technology.

First, we knew that when we upgraded our computer system we would need to upgrade our employees' technical expertise.

We were lucky to have an extensive and excellent MIS staff. Training is mandatory for everyone. Part of each employee's annual evaluation is whether they've completed their required classes. MIS classes are scheduled on an ongoing basis and we have tutorials in the Intelligence Center for those who want to learn more on their own. There is always at least one person on the help desk.

Also, we thought we would have years of computer space. The bane of technology is that as we get more sophisticated it is never big enough and never fast enough. We continue to buy memory, add servers and we hope the Intranet we are developing will make a difference.

Communication

The file server network is only one example of how we use technology. We each have our own virtual phone extension. Each morning, and during the day we need to call in and "change our status." We can be reached — anywhere — through stationary or cellular phones, or on pager. Within the office we also have radio telephones so that our clients and colleagues can reach us even when we are on the move. Some clients have told us we are now more accessible than ever before.

The radio telephones are wonderful. They make us much more reachable than we ever were before. But with it we discovered we needed to learn a new etiquette. For instance, what happens when the phone rings and you're in the bathroom?

How available is appropriate?

There's another issue we needed to think about. Just because we can be reachable everywhere now, should we be reachable in all circumstances? I have been in meetings where each of the participants allows the meeting to be interrupted by phone calls because, "it might be important." This is so frustrating that we now try to make sure everyone in the meeting "goes to pager" before we start. And we won't necessarily respond to the page immediately.

Changing needs
Our telephones and our computer-needs vary during the day and week. At any given time we might need a large screen computer or a small lightweight duo. We can "check out" a laptop or telephone through our concierge. If we just need to check our e-mail, there are electronic drinking fountains throughout the building.

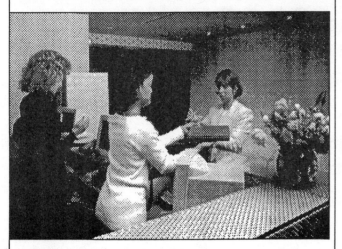

Concierge

KEY FINDINGS AND VARIATIONS ON THE MODELS

So, that is how Virtual Office Team Architecture began, and how we implemented it. Now I want to tell you about our key lessons and the differences and similarities between our office in Los Angeles and our office in New York.

In hindsight, we realized that we had tried to marry two different models, and that the virtual and the team architecture models do not mesh seamlessly. We, and the press focused on how Chiat/Day had become a virtual agency, but that was only half of our paradoxical task.

A virtual office is technology oriented. It requires little or no real estate and means employees can work where ever and whenever you want. What we discovered, however, is that it doesn't enhance collaboration and interaction. In many ways being virtual makes teamwork more difficult.

Team architecture, on the other hand, is relationship oriented. It requires real estate committed to team interaction and collaboration, and it encourages both spontaneous and planned communication.

We discovered that teams are more effective than individuals alone. The quality of our thinking, products and services improved and the need for hands-on management was reduced. Teams, usually working together in project rooms, have increased the sense of unity and communication, and of necessity built an atmosphere of trust, shared vision and responsibilities. The trade-off, we've discovered, seems to be improvement in team communication at the expense of individual productivity.

As it happens, we adopted both models in two offices. The mix was different in each and I'd like to talk about this next. The Cornell University International Workplace Studies Program has called the Venice office a modified virtual office. The New York office it has called a full virtual office. I thought I might be "too close" to our office so I referred to the Cornell University report as well as relied on my own and anecdotal experiences.

The slides I have shown you so far are of the Venice office. Ours is a three story building with project rooms on each floor interspersed with more "static" departments. We found that the multiple floors affected the way we work.

Let me show you a videotape showing the build-out of the New York office. This office was smaller, on one floor, and the virtual culture was more rigorously adhered to because of the space constraints and because Jay Chiat himself would not allow any nesting.

You will see that the architecture in New York is even more amazing than that of the Venice office. You will notice several voice-overs, blending together. These are client testimonials about how well the new office structure worked for them.

show tape (1 min.)

Exterior of Venice office

The rule of thirds

Remember I mentioned the rule of thirds? We thought many employees might spend a third of their time in the office; a third of their time at their home office; and a third of their time in meetings and at other offsite work locations. The rule was actually a riddle, and the answer is, it depends on what your job function is.

Creative teams might work offsite during the developmental stages of creating, but would be in the agency during the other stages. Since creative works on many projects this means they were often onsite. Those who work with research and planning are heavy travelers, so they appreciate the tools for remote work. Media buyers are happy to work most of the time at home. They come in to reconnect with their teams for their very necessary social and visibility needs. Account people, those who are most involved with the business of advertising, spend most of their time either at the office or at the client's office. They need to be visible to nurture and defend the ideas and to monitor the process of the work.

I work at my home office at least one day each week and a couple of hours before coming into the office.

It is the only way I can get some of the more involved projects accomplished.

The time I spend in the office is organized around connecting with my department and the various teams. The research and project work is different in the office than when I work offsite.

In Los Angeles there were so many exciting spontaneous activities happening in the office, people felt they might miss something if they weren't there. It was a fun place to be and they didn't want to leave.

Also, some of the juniors believe it is not okay to work remotely or that they won't learn from their managers. Some people felt if you were working from home the perception was that you might not really be working. As a result, remote work was likely to be bookended around office time in Los Angeles.

New York employees work offsite more often than the Venice employees. This is not only because of the space constraints but because it is perceived as management endorsed. In New York, if you are working at home everyone knows you are working.

Virtual vs. collocated encampments

There were very few dedicated places in New York. Peer pressure, adopted from the outset, discouraged nesting. People worked at home strictly out of necessity.

What was obvious to us in LA was that some people could be more "virtual" than others. For instance, account group assistants would need to remain close to the project rooms. We eventually encouraged encampments close to the team project rooms. The collocation close to the project room is important to the effectiveness of the teams in LA.

Teams

We discovered that there was more interaction and socializing between teams in the smaller, single floor office in New York. The Los Angeles teams were tighter but tended to develop their own mini-cultures. There was less interaction across teams and sometimes even rivalries.

The space

The project rooms are central to the way we work in New York and Los Angeles. They helped team members feel "in the loop." Junior people report that they have much more access to senior people than before. There are some differences though:

— In Los Angeles the teams flocked to the rooms and cycled through all day.
— In New York the rooms were used more formally for meetings or solitary work.

Both Los Angeles and New York have a clubhouse. The clubhouse was intended to be a place for socializing. In LA we have fruit, bagels, and juice in the morning. We have a popcorn and lemonade break at three. Four televisions are on all the time — one is hooked to video games. There are game tables, a pool table and there are punching bags with the faces of senior management on them. The clubhouse in New York has many of the same amenities. It is slightly smaller and has more food and fewer games.

Yet the clubhouse is used very differently in New York than in is in Los Angeles. In New York employees use the clubhouse very purposefully for outreach and visibility as well as to socialize in. In Los Angeles it is one of many places to work alone

Clubhouse -- Los Angeles

or have a meeting in. Some people say it is one of the places they go to pretend to be alone.

The lockers were very useful in New York because of their limited space and because of the weather meant wearing coats and slickers. In Los Angeles, we discovered many people never used their lockers. They would keep their personal possessions in their car or they found places in and around the project rooms to keep their ongoing projects.

One problem we experienced in Los Angeles was that there was no place to get away and think. The Intelligence Center was intended to provide this space but it soon proved to be a work space only marginally more quiet than the rest of the agency. The unexpected density meant that even this space was usually used for work other than research and planning.

Communications

Because of the modified nature of the Los Angeles office we often know where to find each other. In New York there is a greater reliance on the wireless telephone to reach people and most people do not attempt to walk around to find them.

Trust, discipline & boundaries

Having remote capabilities provides us with a freedom, responsibility and a need to trust. I've already mentioned the perception of management endorsement. It also requires discipline of all of us. We not only need to work in a disciplined way; we also need to set reasonable boundaries on our schedules. Just because we now have the tools to work anywhere and anytime, should we? How quickly does our personal life and home blur with our office life? In truth this was harder to adjust to than to learning new computer programs.

TODAY

So, that is how we went "virtual" while working in teams changed how we worked. But nothing is static, and now I'd like to tell you how time and events have altered what we mean by the "virtual office."

In 1995 Chiat/Day merged with TBWA, an agency with a great international presence. The merger has gone exceptionally well even with corporate-culture differences. Our client list leaped. We lost some clients but gained more. The agency as a whole is thriving. The work is great, and ultimately that's what it's about.

The number of employees in the company has jumped, and this has created density problems. In response we added another floor to the New York office and are seeing that they are shifting to a modified setting similar to ours. We expect additional modifications in both offices. Our goal is to provide our staff with the resources to work effectively while removing those things that add unnecessary stress.

The commitment to Team Architecture has grown. We remain enthusiastic about the tools that allow us to be a virtual as we need to be when we need to be. We have taken many of these tools and strategies to our new international offices and continue to look for other tools and models that will allow us to work better.

Not everyone adjusted to the change. It didn't surprise us that some people opted to leave for a place where the offices have doors.

What is interesting though is that many of the people who leave have had trouble adjusting to the constraints of their new jobs. Most people in our office may want a chair, a phone, a computer, and a designated space, but few would want to go back to being alone, losing their freedom, their flexibility and especially their team culture.

THE ROLE OF THE INTELLIGENCE DEPARTMENT

AT TBWA CHIAT DAY

So, that is where we began, how we changed how we worked, and how time altered our plans. Now I'd like to tell you how we do that thing we do in the agency — provide intelligence.

I've already described Offsite Records Management and the Optical Scanning unit. I've talked about the Intelligence Center, the Central Intelligence on the file server, and some of our services.

What I'd like to do is give you some context, philosophy and changes we've experienced.

Chiat/Day had never had a formalized information/ intlligence department before Virtual Team Architecture.

Our promise the agency employees in 1993 and 1994 was that we would provide a collective intelligence superior to the individually hoarded information they had at the time. We've succeeded in that and have now expanded our mission to "providing intelligence, insight and inspiration to the agency." We want to go beyond what we know we know;

TBWA Chiat/Day
Intelligence Department
Mission:

To provide intelligence, insight and inspiration to the agency.

---

beyond what know we don't know; to what we don't know we don't know. We want to be explorers That is a daunting promise.

We provide several levels of service: end-user, ready reference, information or data dissemination, intelligence products, and proactive services. Most of these are pretty self-explanatory, but I'd like to take a couple of moments to talk about three of them: end-user products, intelligence products, and proactive services.

People in general often make rational decisions to defer research to others, however, our time is limited and we have found that we need to be selective about appropriate projects. Our goal with the end-user products is to give our employees tools to do their own initial research and to think through what it is they really need to know. We want them to have thought about and explored their questions so that we can help them be more strategic in their solutions.

We provide access to information through such resources as commercial databases and the internet, CD-ROMs, the library, syndicated research, and reports on the file server, and Intranet. We also provide end-user online databases such as the InSite service, and hope to increase some of these subscriptions.

The research our intelligence group performs usually includes analysis and key insights. When possible we provide intelligence reports. I don't want to make this sound simple. Many of our reports take around 30 hours to produce and some have taken over 80 hours. But by providing intelligence rather than a large stack of "stuff," we have become a part of the strategic team rather than one of the service/response departments.

Although these reports are usually in response to a direct request, we try to make many of our insights available to others. It is amazing how many strategic requests stimulate similar projects.
Some of our work is proactive. This includes a daily awareness program that goes out over our e-mail and Intranet. We have prepared press and award databases for our Internet site and we post reports and "think pieces" on the file server.

We also locate and publish "best of" recommendations and reports prepared by our account planners and by others in the agency, including ourselves. We distribute this package in hard copy to key people in our agency network, making sure we acknowledge those who contribute. We have had raves about this product and it has increased our visibility throughout the network.

You may notice that I said we distribute this as hard copy. I'm a great believer in providing intelligence in formats that are easily accessible. For some that is electronic. That would often be easiest for us. For many people, even in our forward-thinking offices, a hard copy is still the easiest to read, and I have come to realize that easy usage and high visibility is often more important than politically-correct dissemination.

Today, the Intelligence Department is critical to the agency network. Business is bustling and we get requests from all of our client teams, and most of the agency offices inthe U.S. and International. Requests come to us through e-mail, fax and phone calls. Our department has been instrumental in helping the agency get new business and do better work for our existing clients. I believe that this will only increase.

We've noticed that the quality of the requests we get has changed in the past three years. We still get those "tell us everything there is to know about industry X" requests, but we now also get deeper, more interesting, questions and we are usually asked to contribute what we think are the most significant leverage points to help us help the client.

We have some of the smartest people in the advertising business at our agency. And when we are able to get beyond the obvious questions and answers we can find solutions for our clients' marketing problems that will change the way they work.

CONCLUSION
I've given you a lot of information today. I've talked about how, in 1993 and 1994 we plunged into the unknown, knowing we needed to change the way we worked to be successful. I've told you what our process was and how our key lessonnmeant that we needed to take the best tools of the virtual office model and marry it to the best of team architecture.

I've described the differences between the Los Angeles and the New York offices. I discussed some of the changes our agency experienced in the past three-four years and how these are affecting us. Finally, I talk about how we provide intelligence at the agency.

I know I went over the listed half hour and I'd love to answer your questions. But before that I'd like to thank you, and especially Barbara Robinson. In preparing for today, I had a chance to review the process again, more thoroughly than ever before, and I see how far we've come. That is a gift. Thank you.

velda_ruddock@tbwachiat.com

WHEN THE PLACE YOU WORK IS THE WORLD

Linda M. McFadden
Presented at the SLA State-of-the-Art Institute
The Virtual Workplace: One Size Doesn't Fit All
November 7-8, 1996

Introduction

I think the title of my presentation might sound a little ambitious and a little arrogant.
After all, the world is a big place and, quite frankly, I haven't visited all of it yet. So let
me explain this audacious claim.

I worked for a relatively small company of about 6000 employees for eighteen years, but
Herman Miller, Inc., has been an incredibly cosmopolitan kind of company since at least
1930 and a global market player since the 1950s. And while my only forays outside of the
U. S. so far have been minimal, I have been involved for some time in an international
network of colleagues who see their work and clients through a worldview lens and from
a systems perspective. By systems perspective, I mean to say with an acute awareness of
the interrelationship of THINGS, tangible and intangible—work and play, man made and
natural, here and there, now and then.

And so I have come to believe that we all now work *in the world* in a very different sense
than I might have defined that ten years ago—and that is whether you work for a
corporation, a public library, a hospital, or as an independent consultant.

With that perspective in mind, over the next 30 minutes I would like to speak about four specific areas of activity that have been involved or will be involved in the unfolding of a new work order that has no respect for old boundaries:

- First, I would like to weave together for you the design and management philosophies and history at Herman Miller, Inc., to show how they worked together to prepare Herman Miller and me for a radically changing world.

- Second, I will describe Herman Miller's response and my own as corporate librarian and communications manager to the alternative work strategies emerging in the 1990s and the new relationships between work process and work place.

- Third, I'll elaborate somewhat on my personal experiences and reflections as a new member of a virtual work community.

- Finally, I'd like to get into some possible implications for libraries and librarians.

Sound ambitious? I think so too. So let me get started and see where I end up.

Herman Miller, Inc.

Herman Miller had been established in 1905 by a small group of investors in the tiny, Dutch immigrant town of Zeeland, Michigan. While initially a run-of-the-mill manufacturer of princess dressers for The Sears Roebuck Company, by the 1950s it had already achieved significant recognition as an innovative problem solving company of critically acclaimed designs. This company was special.

- Its facilities were exquisite.

- Its furniture designs by the 1970s were considered the most innovative in the industry.

- Its management practices were revolutionary and included its people practices, environmental policies and even its philanthropy.

In each of these areas, it has won numerous and prestigious awards for years from every quarter of the globe.

This company was truly extraordinary and one of the few "learning organizations"[1] out there, and I was lucky to be a part of it.

As corporate librarian and archivist from about 1976 to 1986, and then, in addition, communications manager and organizational change catalyst in the late 1980s through 1995, I was in the most fortunate position to conduct oral histories with many of the early designers and Mr. De Pree while they were still alive, and have had a relatively close working relationship with senior management on an ongoing basis. From them I learned a great deal about the role that business can play in the world.

Dirk Jan De Pree (affectionately known as D. J. to everyone), CEO from 1923-1960, taught me about the early days of challenge and response, of chaos and emerging order, which Mr. De Pree would simply call God's providence. When the company was faltering during the depression, D. J. made himself vulnerable to the teachings and perspectives of a New York City man by the name of Gilbert Rhode. Rhode convinced D. J. to completely "reinvent" Herman Miller by going "modern" in 1930 and adopting the principles that design must be honest and that furniture should serve the people who used it . Without a doubt this flew in the face of the "planned obsolescence" principle of new product design and introductions being followed by the rest of the industry at the time.

Following Rhode's untimely death in 1940, Mr. De Pree found *George Nelson*, an architect and designer in New York, who was dreaming about radical new approaches to interior environments. In addition to his own unique contributions to our understanding of the work place, Nelson was a great teacher about the value of diversity. Specifically, he brought to the company the diversity of genius in the other great designers of the 40s and 50s.

---

[1] I use Peter Senge's definition of a learning organization: One with the capacity to create its own future.

Ray and Charles Eames, a creative husband and wife team, taught me and the world about "good goods" and that good design could be an exquisite match of technology and art, as their famous lounge chair and other renowned products so ably illustrate.

Alexander Girard, the genius behind Herman Miller's extraordinary textiles in the 1950s and 1960s, also introduced playfulness into the working environments through folk art and unusual visual imagery. He taught us all that good design is universal and exists in the shop stalls of folk artists around the world as well as in the studios of companies like Herman Miller and Knoll International.

The later designers were just as instructive and inspiring.

Robert Propst showed us how to leverage what we were learning about participative work processes and innovative product design to develop what has been known commonly for years as Action Office, the first U. S. "open plan" design for office furniture. His ideas were carried to a new level by other designers with the introduction of Ethospace Interiors.

William Stumpf introduced the whole concept of ergonomics into the workplace with his extraordinary seating, the Ergon line, then Equa and most recently the Aeron chair. Other designers were and still are important teachers. Don Chadwick partnered with Stumpf in the two most recent seating lines. Bruce Burdick's high-tech furniture was still on display at the Epcot Center the last time I was there several years ago.

Just as important as the influence these designers had on the company's good fortune and fame, however, were it's management practices. Carl Frost ("Jack Frost" to Herman Miller employees) helped Mr. D. J. DePree and his son Hugh introduce into the company in 1950 the Scanlon Plan of participative management and its principles of identity, participation, equity and competence. There is a quote from D. J. which is inscribed on a small wall sculpture at Herman Miller: "A business is rightly judged by its product and service, but it must also face scrutiny and judgment as to its humanity." D. J.'s belief in the extraordinary abilities of human beings coupled with Frost's principles of participation guided the work of Herman Miller in everything it did for years and years, even into the years of its greatest innovations. They were practicing Theory Y management before the phrase was coined by Douglas McGregor. Jack Frost was so highly regarded and dearly loved by the employees of Herman Miller that they chipped in and bought him to car to replace the old jalopy he drove weekly from Lansing to Zeeland to be with the company as it forged it's future.

Commitment to good design, to honesty in all that it did, and to the principles that human beings wish to do good work and make a difference in the world and are multi-dimensional in their talents and abilities —these foundational values were good preparation for the rapid change we are experiencing today.

Business Information and Communication Services

I will say unashamedly that I was a sponge during my entire career at Herman Miller—soaking up the wisdom, experiences and imaginings of each of these heroes and many others both internally and externally related to this great enterprise. As best I could, I tried to keep up in my own arenas of responsibility.

The library evolved from a physical to a virtual collection, providing ever increasing quality and responsiveness of service without adding staff.

Internal communications relied more and more on alternative media channels which were more timely and in some ways more effective than a primary reliance on print, including video productions, face-to-face extravaganzas, videoconferencing, and electronic networking.

Eventually, I was also heavily involved in introducing new ways of doing business beyond information retrieval or communications processes, including

- Leading the introduction of TQM tools and methods and systems thinking into our corporate environment, helping to create a "learning organization"

- Leading a "data warehousing" project, which allowed me to use all of my accumulated library, communications and quality backgrounds in an entirely new field of marketing communications that would basically revolutionize how the industry would communicate with customers

- Leading the company into the arena of internet and intranet use

Then, in the mid 90s, I was asked to serve on three teams of particular relevance to our subject matter today:

- The *Workplace Integration Team* looked internally as Herman Miller's use of space and facilities to determine how it might best learn from and model for clients new workplace strategies.

- The *Home Officing* team was establishing a pilot program along with recommended policies and practices for telecommuting within the Herman Miller organization.

- The *Employee Information Library* team was seeking the technology to create a library of information by and about Herman Miller employees that would support real-time, employee initiated information retrieval independent of geographic location.

Each of these teams were working to help Herman Miller understand and act on the ongoing changes in the workplace, which brings me to Herman Miller's still emerging response to the requirements of a virtual work environment.

The Virtual Workplace

Herman Miller and the rest of the office furniture industry has been in a deep study about the possibilities of a virtual workplace for some time, funding much of the research in one way or another. After all, if they didn't get it right, they were simply going to be out of business. Herman Miller, for example, figured out that their own offices were empty 60-70% of the time. Just figure out what that means in unjustified "fixed" office furniture and equipment expense to a company!

As a result of their research, their own experience with the practices of TQM, process improvement and concurrent engineering, Herman Miller could see that significant new patterns of working were emerging. By 1994, Herman Miller proposed that there were new kinds of teams in operation in the corporate environment and, with them, new kinds of work space requirements.[2]

Linear teams, with people in well-defined roles performing routine, repetitive tasks such as order entry, inventory control and loan processing, require **permanent assigned spaces** dedicated to support individual work that is passed "down the line" so to speak, with some needed cooperation. By the way, these spaces seem to correspond to what the Institute for the Future called "Caves and Commons" spaces—an interesting choice of terms.

Parallel teams are usually multi-disciplinary or cross functional and are assembled temporarily for a project that requires different specialized skills from each member. These are the kinds of teams involved in concurrent engineering of new product. They may very well need **group address spaces** which are not assigned to a particular functional team but are available for group use as needed.

Closely related and also temporary are **circular teams** specifically created for innovation on an *ad hoc* basis. While they exist, these teams may expand and contract. People come and go as a project evolves. These teams could "rent" a place called **tenant space.**

In addition, alternative settings for meetings were identified:

- **videoconferencing rooms** to support the special lighting, acoustical, and technological requirements of video broadcasts and group

- **huddle spaces** for informal meetings, chance encounters, and work breaks to foster idea exchange and communication, and

- **learning spaces,** which can range from traditional classrooms to multipurpose rooms designed to support participative learning experiences like team-building. I think corporate libraries might fit into this category.

---

[2] The definitions which follow are taken from a variety of sources, including "Evolutionary Workplaces" (Zeeland, MI: Herman Miller, 1996) and *Rethinking the Workplace* (Menlo Park, CA: Institute for the Future, 1995).

New alternative *individual* work styles and their facility solutions were also identified:

- **Hoteling provides** unassigned individual work spaces for use by a particular individual for a specified block of time, with a corporate "concierge" responsible for scheduling and preparing spaces for use as needed.

- **Free address** work spaces, on the other hand, are unassigned and can be used by anyone in the company as needed on a on a first-come, first-served basis.

- **Just-in-time** spaces are left as open and flexible as possible by providing mobile or easily moved furniture and screens or partitions that can be assembled to support individual work processes "on the spot."

- **Shared assigned** refers to a situation where two or more employees are assigned to use the same desk, office, or workstation at different times, as in a "job share" situation.

- **Permanent assigned** (traditional) spaces are required for those individuals who continue to need an office space permanently assigned to them because most of their process oriented work is performed on-site.

Finally, and in addition to these corporate solutions is what is commonly known as **telecommuting** or **telework** where employees or sole proprietors like myself work at home, in a **neighborhood business center**, or out of their **cars**.

Of course, all of the furniture manufacturers are offering suggestions as to ideal conditions for telework or telecommuting from a corporate perspective. In a very recent article focusing on Herman Miller's pilot home officing program, but also mentioning Steelcase and Haworth, the following kinds of jobs were identified as "best" for telecommuting:

- An information-based job that doesn't rely on resources at the main office—or one in which resources can be reached electronically (which is libraries come in)
- Work that has clear, measurable objectives and doesn't require close supervision
- One in which face-to-face contacts can be scheduled in advance.

Herman Miller also suggests the best ways to make telecommuting work:

- A home office should be a dedicated space where work-in-progress won't be disturbed.
- Family, friends and neighbors have to understand that when you're home, you're working, not waiting to chat over coffee.
- Someone else should be responsible for young children or the care of the elderly parent; working at home is not a substitute for such care.
- Don't use telecommuting as an excuse to avoid meetings back at the main office. Make yourself available—and visible—on a regular basis so co-workers won't resent you and bosses won't forget you.
- Keep to a regular schedule. Remember that your work will be scrutinized more than usual, so don't miss deadlines.[3]

---

[3] "Home Alone," *The Grand Rapids Press*, Sunday, October 6, 1996: F1, F5.

At the time I was involved in this work and figuring out what Herman Miller should do internally with its own employees as well as what it should be focusing on externally in terms of its clients, I was trying to figure out just where I was.

I served on a parallel team and a circular team. I had a special project room for the parallel team I led and met off-site for most of the circular teams I served on. My "linear team," which I might equate to a functional team, met in on-demand meeting rooms about once a month. Otherwise, each member was fairly autonomous, and I really didn't even see why our offices had to be located close to each other at all anymore.

Personally, I wanted a "free address" or "hotel" corporate space with a primary emphasis on work out of a home office. I basically volunteered to be sent home to work. Guess what? I was, but not in a way I had intended.

Membership in a Virtual Work Community

Indeed, when I went "home to work," it was not as a corporate employee. I look my severance package and allowed myself the opportunity and challenge to do what I had dreamed of doing for the prior two years: working as an independent consultant with a network of colleagues and clients interested in organizational change that would be principles based and beneficial to society. More on that tomorrow.

While the office furniture industry has been very helpful in mapping out ways that companies like Chiat/Day and AT&T could create necessary conditions for alternative work strategies for their own employees and their larger networks of contract and consulting partners, it has been to date less helpful for those engaged in the kind of work I am doing today. But let me start with the easier challenges I faced.

Given what I knew about alternative work strategies, I really was quite ready to tackle my home office as soon as I made the decision to go off on my own. I had a room with some built in furniture, including two bunkbeds which work well for posters, flip charts, paper supplies, and Christmas gifts as they accumulate over the year. I had a beautiful Herman Miller roll top desk large enough for my computer monitor, phone and left-handed space for paper work. I converted a closet into a bookcase. I had business cards, letter-head and other materials quickly available. I upgraded my technology—new computer with all of the power and peripherals one might need to electronically connect anywhere in the world. A super-duper fax, scanner, copier. A laser printer. A new business line and voice mail. I maintained my fee-based on-line accounts and signed up with the local freenet for Internet access and e-mail.

This was all the easy stuff. The harder part was the interpersonal stuff. My best friends became my phone, e-mail, and my fax machine. They are not very personable, to tell you the truth, and tended to create new phobias: telephonebillphobia, computervirusphobia, and claustrophobia. I had to invent ways of getting fresh air and finding warm bodies to talk to and be with besides my loving Golden Lab, Sam. I fit exercise and outdoor time into my work with clients both in town and out. I love working from my home, but I do need to work hard on finding *non-virtual* ways of being with people.

So I have physical issues—my space and equipment—and I have psychological/social issues. But the biggest issue of all, the one I think about the most, is mastering an entirely new way of working, one I'll call *collaboration* for lack of a better word, which involves and requires working with others without any organizational authority or structure for the purpose of creating something new and different and of benefit for more than any of the individuals or organizations involved separately and alone. It is an issue that still requires a lot of research and one in which the office furniture industry has not demonstrated much interest, probably because of its incredible complexity and implications for the industry's own sales process and potential revenues. It is also the area that could have major implications for new roles for librarians and libraries.

The Institute for the Future warned that

> "Most firms today . . .are experimenting with giving people flexibility in their work locations without much change in the structure of work." Whereas, "The challenge is to connect the location-dependent and -independent pieces of the organization within the shared electronic space and structure ways they can leverage each other.

By 2005, more firms will integrate multilocational work with new ways of conducting collaborative work in both electronic and physical spaces; this conjunction will redefine business altogether. In general, what we now see as fairly separate options will evolve together to create the integrated virtual office."[4]

This integrated virtual office for me means collaborating with consultants from multiple disciplines—including graphic designers, OD consultants, information systems specialists, and librarians—from all over the world, electronically and face-to-face, around projects, events, and learnings, completely outside the boundaries of any one organization. We are highly dependent on one another without having any authority or hierarchical or even direct monetary control over each other. We are bonded through our principles, vision and professional interests.

I asked some of my collaborators about their challenges working in an integrated virtual workplace.

Their concerns mirror many of my own about space, support, relationships, etc. In particular I appreciate the remarks and insights of my friend Stas' from Ann Arbor who "collaborated" on a major client project located in New Orleans with me and others from as far away as the United Kingdom:

---

[4]Institute for the Future, "Mapping the Future of the Virtual Office," *Rethinking the Workplace* (Menlo Park, CA: Institute for the Future, 1995), 211.

Being virtual does not preclude, or take care of the non-virtual behavior of

excluding people from meetings, conversations, work, etc. Leaving people off the

distribution list, ignoring their responses, has the same effect that it does in the real

workplace. You can't collaborate if you aren't there ("there" virtually speaking). .

. . .I find it very difficult to get my thoughts straightened out talking to myself. . . .I

believe that the key for collaboration to work in the virtual is to make sure that

there is frequent feedback on inputs and outputs. There is nothing more

frustrating for me than to send something out on the airwaves and not get any

response at all.

Stas' seems to be getting at exactly what William Schrage describes in *No More Teams?*
when he talks about striving to create networks of shared spaces that are not physical in
nature.

"Designing for collaboration means that the emphasis shifts from networks of

information distribution and transmission to networks of shared spaces. The

question no longer is, 'What do I do with this?' but 'Who else should see this so I

can understand and use this better?' The issue isn't just processing information—

it's creating information with others."[5]

Even when speaking strictly about a corporate internal environment, in a survey conducted
by Collaborative Strategies of 100 companies, representing multiple industries excluding

computer hardware and software development, 83% indicated that collaboration was critical to the function of their businesses.[6] Collaborative Strategies goes on to indicate the kinds of collaborative work being supported by internet and intranet applications:

- Document management

- Group calendaring/scheduling

- Project management

- Communication, and

- Knowledge management

I don't know about you, but this sounds like it might have some serious implications for librarians and anyone else with traditional responsibilities for the collection, management, analysis and distribution of information.

Implications of the virtual workplace for librarians and for libraries.

I teach a Sunday School class for preschoolers called "Children in Worship." Perhaps some of you are familiar with it. We dramatize stories from the Bible using a variety of

---

[5] Schrage, Michael, *No More Teams! Mastering the Dynamics of Creative* Collaboration (New York: Currency Doubleday, 1996), 149.
[6] "Electronic Collaboration on the Internet and Intranets" (San Francisco, Collaborative Strategies, 1996) (http:www.collaborate.com)

props, and then pose "wondering" questions to the children that do not require their specific answers but are meant to prompt their thinking about implications of the story.

Let us imagine that what I have just told you is in fact a story that is unfolding, one for which we do not yet have an ending. I would like us to "wonder" together. Believe me, I claim no answers.

First of all, let's ponder the whole concept of "library" and "librarian" in a corporation that has gone "virtual" or in a collaborative community without walls. I wonder what skills might no longer be needed? What new skills need to be developed? What about the growing numbers of consultants, individuals collaborating either completely outside the corporate or institutional environment, or interacting with members inside those environments. How might librarians help them? How might they help Stas' make sure his messages and connections don't get lost in Cyberspace? Or is that someone else's problem entirely? I wonder?

According to Schrage,

> "Successful collaborators are constantly on the lookout for people and information that will help them achieve their mission, but they do so on their own terms.... .Successful collaborators rarely hesitate to establish links—if not ties—to other people who can provide either specific doses of necessary information or useful insights to guide the collaborative effort. These outsiders rarely become an

ongoing part of the collaborative process, but they do serve specific functional roles at critical junctures in that process."[7]

I wonder if we might consider this statement by Schrage a serious and attractive challenge to librarians? I wonder if we might not only become the people who help link collaborators to the information that will help them achieve their mission, but go beyond Schrage's expectations and truly become a part of the collaborative process. I wonder *how* we can do that if in fact we assume (and why not?) that we *can and should*?

I collaborate daily as an independent consultant on organizational change strategies, but my librarian "persona" is always with me and always in operation. If I can see what it brings to the party, is there a way to let others see and act on that? I participate in an electronic conferencing system dedicated to a select group of OD consultants. I am a little more active than others, I think, because of my broad "librarian" knowledge about information resources. I wonder if it might not be possible for librarians in all sectors of society to leverage their diverse knowledge, experiences, and talents as a fulcrum into collaborative relationships that will allow them to then demonstrate their value as information professionals?

In the evolution towards the integrated virtual office, in the work that needs to be done to change work process as well as work space and technology, I wonder will librarians have a role? I ask this of communications professionals as well. The Institute for the Future

---

[7] Schrage, p. 164.

lists as a major issue needing attention as we move forward the "massive investment in knowledge infrastructure by business."

> Knowledge will be embodied in people and systems. Developing business cultures, processes, and people to create new knowledge and manage existing knowledge will be critical to the business world of the late 1990s. Knowledge management is likely to succeed reengineering as the business mantra of the next decade. But what does it mean? How will it be valued? And how do you convince shareholders of that value?[8]

Those of you who are figuring this out and helping it along have a great deal to offer the rest of us who are wondering "how."

In my own state of Michigan librarians of all types are forging new and exciting forms of collaboration. Our library cooperatives, formed to promote multi-type library cooperation, have been aggressively playing a role. While the public libraries get most of the credit, it really is a cooperative effort. See the 1996 special issue of *Library Hi Tech*, "State of the State Reports." In it, just one effort in Michigan illustrates new forms of collaboration led by librarians:

> In the heart of Michigan's remote upper peninsula is a community networking project called Walden III. This project, conceived by the Mid-Peninsula Library

Cooperative in Iron Mountain, includes total community involvement and specifically provides for connectivity among public libraries, local governments, medical, business, and professional communities. Central to Walden III is the concept that access to digital information is critical to the twenty-first-century community—and that public libraries are key partners in the process.[9]

I wonder about our traditional library facilities. I was pleased to find on the Internet a paper entitled "How to Study and Design for Collaborative Browsing in the Digital Library" which describes the issues librarians need to be concerned about in this whole arena. For example, the author posits that "traditional systems are mostly designed to support individual users" which will, when "extended to a digital library. . .lead us to construct an entire virtual library for each user which they can wander around entirely alone." The paper goes on to describe positive approaches that digital libraries can take which "offers the opportunity for far greater and more diverse kinds of collaboration than are possible in physical libraries."[10]

I wonder about our need for identity? Do we even want to be included in a broader collaborative effort, to not only join the new ways of working, but to lead. Librarians are often identified as early adopters. This time, perhaps we shouldn't just be early adopters,

---

[8] Institute for the Future, "The Best of Times, the Worst of Times: Income Distribution in the Knowledge Economy," *Rethinking the Workplace* (Menlo Park, CA: Institute for the Future, 1995), p. 227.
[9] Palmer, Eileen M., "Michigan: Building Electronic Community Information Centers: Public Libraries," *Library Hi Tech*, Consecutive Issue 54-55, v. 14, Number 2-3 (1996), p. 165.
[10] Twidale, Michael, "How to study and design for collaborative browsing in the digital library," Computing Department, Lancaster University, LA1 4YR UK, 1995. (http://atgl.wustl.edu:80/DL94/paper/levy.html)

which isn't a bad reputation to have, but to be inventors as well. I've been observing a dialogue going on in SLA Library Management Division's Listserve about whether or not the Special Libraries Association should be renamed. I sympathize with the differing positions. Many feel that they want the label librarian, that it is understood, that it keeps us from getting confused with "them." Others feel trapped by the label and want to find another. I wish I had an answer for you. I can tell you that in my current role I don't want any "specialized" labels, not even OD consultant, because of the limited stereotypes associated with any existing job descriptions.

I saw that SLA was advertising another program, "Getting Out of the Box." Did any of you attend? How many of you want to get out of the Box? I think there is more opportunity to do that now than ever before. Indeed, I fear that those who desperately want to stay in the box will find themselves in obsolete positions soon. We are in a revolution, a major one.

Conclusion

For quite a while I fretted about how I would conclude this presentation. I have wandered over a period of twenty years of my life, multiple careers, complex and still emerging concepts of work. I've paced back and forth between my role as librarian and my vision for my new work. I've probably posed far more questions than I have answered. Indeed, I haven't really come up with any conclusions, have I? So I think I can only end with an invitation to the dialogue about where we go from here, hopefully having added some new

perspective through my own "wonderings."

References:

Collaborative Strategies. "Electronic Collaboration on the Internet and Intranets."
Collaborative Strategies, 1996. (http:www.collaborate.com)

"Evoluntionary Workplaces." Zeeland, MI: Herman Miller, Inc., 1996.

The Herman Miller Catalog. Zeeland, MI: Herman Miller, Inc., 1948.

"Home Alone." *The Grand Rapids Press* Sunday, October 6, 1996: F1, F5.

Institute for the Future. "The Best of Times, the Worst of Time: Income Distribution in
the Knowledge Economy.*" Rethinking the Workplace.* Menlo Park, CA: Institute for the
Future, 1995: 223-228.

Institute for the Future. "Mapping the Future of the Virtual Office." *Rethinking the
Workplace.* Menlo Park, CA: Institute for the Future, 1995: 205-213.

Institute for the Future. "Work+Family+Information Technology=???" Menlo Park, CA:
Institute for the Future, 1995: 215-222.

"Nelson, Eames, Girard, Propst: The Design Process at Herman Miller." Edited by
Mildred S. Friedman. *Design Quarterly* 98/99. Milwaukee: The Walker Art Center,
1975.

Palmer Eileen M. "Michigan: Building Electronic Community Information Centers:
Public Libraries." *Library Hi Tech* Consecutive Issue 54-55, v. 14, Number 2-3 (1996):
163-167 (Special Issue on State of the State Reports)

Schrage, Michael. *No More Teams! Mastering the Dynamics of Creative Collaboration.*
New York: Currency Doubleday, 1996.

Twidale, Michael, Computing Department, Lancaster University. "How to Study and
Design for Collaborative Browsing in the Digital Library." 37th Allerton Institute,
Graduate School of Library and Information Science, University of Illinois at Urbana-
Champaign, Monticello, Illinois, October 29-31, 1995.
(http://atgl.wustl.edu:80/DL94/paper/levy.html)

THE VIRTUAL ORGANIZATION
NEW CHALLENGES AND OPPORTUNITIES FOR INFORMATION SPECIALISTS

A DEFINITION

There are a variety of ways to define a virtual organization. For this presentation I want to use this a fairly simplistic definition. A Virtual Organization is an organization without geographic boundaries and has the ability to operate seamlessly whether there are plant locations in a state, located across a country or located in several countries. This is an organization that recognizes that in order to operate competitively it must provide its employees with the capability to access needed internal company information regardless of the day or hour. Employees also need to be able to have other information needs for external information handled expeditiously.

THE EVOLUTION OF THE VIRTUAL ORGANIZATION

Science fiction authors in the late 40's started creating virtual workplaces and virtual communities in their books. Initially many of these ideas presented in these fiction books seemed fanciful. In the following decades fiction started to become fact as space travel became a reality and new products with practical business applications started to be marketed from the embryonic computer industry. By the late 80's electronic cottage industries and telecommuting had become a way of doing business for many companies and individuals. The rapid improvements in the computer technology which saw the migration from main frames to networked personal computers with enhanced capabilities, greater reliability and the ability to customize the systems made the dream of operating successful virtual corporation within reach of almost every business.

The business world started to deal with the need to restructure, downsize or rightsize in order to become more competitive. The end result was smaller work forces and in scattered locations as the need to become global became an important economic strategy. The ability to implement reliable computer networks to let the remaining staff to become more productive became a key business strategy with the recognition that productivity could only be achieved if information to do various tasks was readily available.

While companies were somewhat wary of the constant Internet hype as an reliable method to be implemented as a business process, the ability to transfer files, to be able to send or receive communications around the clock made economic sense and to be able to access various information sources began to make converts. The next logical business decision was to develop personal networks called Intranets while worrying about system security.

This is the environment that successful and innovative information specialists must work, achieving the status as an information resource partner for all units of the organization.

ADAPTATION OF LIBRARY SERVICES TO THIS NEW ENVIRONMENT

Information specialists have long been involved in developing many of the computer hardware and software products for organizing and accessing data files. Many corporate and government agency librarians were in the position to provide major input in the development some of the products as the need to create structured files became obvious and this was a competency that librarians had   New partnerships were soon being formed between systems people and information specialists. The challenges that this offered to many librarians lead many to become information theory experts which evolved into a new field of study.

There are many examples that can be presented highlighting how librarians have implemented technology in this new era of information networks. Here are a few examples of these activities:

Networked Catalogs: Libraries like most businesses have for years operated as single entities or as a system with branches where connectivity was handled by telephone or book trucks. To improve access to collections in other libraries printed union list of serials, book catalogs and bibliographies were created using a lot of labor. The development and availability of OCLC services at first regionally, nationally and then internationally followed by the ability to acquire stand alone networked systems which could connect to other networked systems to the adoption of Internet as a library service serves as examples of how librarians have used new computer technology to prove improved services for their clientele.

Standards: The need for standards in the computer industry became obvious as more companies started acquiring the technology for their overall business operations and found that other purchased systems were not compatible. Librarians had recognized very early in the development of their field that their needed to be standards in order to provide access and the adoption such standards as the different cataloging codes is one example. Each new code came about as a result of new formats which were not provided for in older codes. However as some of the early computer systems were acquired, libraries like many businesses were caught buying incompatible technology. The Beta vs. VHS technology option is a reminder that good business decisions can still result in making a long-term incorrect purchasing decision.

Librarians who want to take advantage of the computer technology quickly realized that they had to become a voice in developing standards for those products that they would be using. They also realized that they needed to work more closely with the various vendors to provide the type of product which would meet the needs of the library community. Many companies that now develop products for this market seek panels of libraries when products are in the beta testing stages. Librarians are also participating in greater numbers as panel members of various standard committees like ANSI.

Resource Sharing Ventures: Initially it was the large academic research libraries that took advantage of accessing other libraries collections using systems like ARLIN and OCLC to identify their collections' strengthens and weaknesses. This information was then incorporated into their collection development policy. As the costs of various library materials started to rapidly escalate, particularly scientific literature, and budgets for library materials were leveling off or decreasing , many librarians started developing cooperative collection development agreements. More recently, multitype regional cooperatives have been established and have become networked providing the increased opportunities for cooperative collection development for books and access to various nonprint periodical databases. Both technology and new economic realities have facilitated the rapid development of these new cooperative networks. Other cooperative are being implemented with the latest emphasis promoting Internet access by providing training opportunities for staff and library users.

The Internet as a Resource: Each new generation of technology have seen librarians rapidly adapting their services to take full advantage of the new technology to provide new and improved services for their users. The Internet is the latest service which has been adopted by libraries as one of the services they offer. This is was not a case of jumping onto the band wagon but looking at this technology recognizing that the promises were partially just hype and determining what elements of the Internet needed to be made available from their libraries. Many librarians have submitted suggestions for changes in structure, others have created products with quality information to be mounted on the Internet and used by others.

Many libraries had at least one or two doubting Thomas's who were feeling stressed out due to budget cutbacks and reduction in the number of staff and wanted nothing to do with this very amorphous information source. The original chat rooms and other listservs were not of much interest, but it did not take long for listservs of particular interest to librarians to be mounted on the Internet. Many now find these library listservs serve as additional staff member providing in many instances very fast respond time to a query for a specific bit of information, provide quick analysis on how good a product is or advice on how to solve a glitch in one of your nonprint sources. They also serve as a forum for year around discussion of various information issues rather than just relying on annual conferences and publications from professional associations.

The Role of Intranet: There have been a lot of concerns expressed about the content of many Internet resources, the reliability of the Internet, the security of the Internet and the speed of accessing certain resources on the Internet, but the potential of the Internet as an information resource and a communication device has won over many converts. The popularity of the Internet is now causing access problems and the time involved to get to particular sites is becoming a problem. The pluses and minuses of the Internet have been weighed carefully by many organizations and many have decided to utilize the concept by creating their own private networks called Intranets. Organizations have also recognized that the Internet has become a marketing device and have developed sites which can be assessed on the Web.

The rapid adoption of the Internet and the Intranet by organizations have created new demands for the expertise of information specialists.

REASONS FOR THESE CHANGES

Increased Reliability and Capability of the Technology: The availability of dependable, upgradable and affordable technology has been the biggest influence in impacting the way business is conducted. It is technology which has made the virtual organization a reality. Those who have rapidly adapted to the kaleidoscope technology products to create and produce their products and to improve customer service have seen their competitive edge increase and improved profits.

Customer Expectations: In today's business environment the customer is demanding more product for their dollar and they expect to receive better and more specialized service. Customers have many options on how to expend their money seek consistent product quality and good customer service before expending any money. The customer has become a major factor in determining business practices.

The Changing Business Climate: The global economy has generate more competitors for the customer's dollar and time. Deregulation has provided additional competitors. Environmental concerns and the resulting "greening" of many business activities have resulted in new ways of conducting business. Many economic activities are now monitored on a twenty-four hour basis, the phrase "banker hours" has an entirely different meaning than it did in the early 80's. All of this has lead to increase demands for more timely information for decision making activities so the business can remain competitive.

New Information Suppliers as Direct Competitors: Alvin Toffler and John Naisbett were among the early business gurus to promote the concept that we as an economy were moving from the Industrial Age to the Information Age. As more and more business gurus started to promote this new Information Economy in terms of potential monetary rewards for those who structured their business to meet this new paradigm. Others quickly became very interested in becoming creators of "information products". The word "Information" quickly became a highly marketable term in conjunction with many of the new products, processes and training opportunities being sold. As information specialists we are beginning to find ourselves in a very crowded field trying to get the attention of both our customers and our bosses. This has meant that efforts have had to be expended in differentiate between what they are providing as information products and services and what information specialists provide as information services.

As experts in the information field we very aware that most people do not have good information seeking skills and they often accept the first remotely suitable piece of information as a suitable answer to their query. Our problem is now to make ourselves visible in this sea of competitors as a source for quick, timely and accurate information.

TRADITIONAL COMPETENCIES

Let's take a few minutes to review some of the traditional competencies or skill sets that are typically associated with librarians.

- **Gatekeeper** The protector and guardian of the integrity collection
- **Organizer** Provide access to materials by logically organizing material
- **Indexer** Developer structured theasuri to process access to contents
- **Searcher** Ability to identify needed information
- **Retriever** Ability to get needed information
- **Archivist** Obtains significant historical material for retention

These are important skill sets and form the backbone of how many of the newer information software packages have been structured. These skills have established the parameters that successful information products must operate within. Many of the new software packages can do many of the more mechanical or gross functions of these jobs. The success that has been achieved in searching multiple databases with a single search strategy has been achieved by careful implementation to the basic rules that we mastered as *Organizers, Indexers and Searchers.*

NEW COMPETENCIES

In today's world there are many new competencies or skill sets which information specialists can bring to the workplace. These competencies have been stated in the 1996 Special Libraries Association publication entitled *Competencies for Special Librarians of the 21st Century.* My interpretation of these new competencies expected of today's information specialists are:

- *Evaluators* A critical skill with the plethora of resources now available in various formats
- *Trainers* To develop and maintain the skills of your clientele in using information resources
- *Educators* To teach the need of effective information strategies in making decisions
- *Mediators* Between the product developers and the end user needs
- *Marketers* Promoters of their services and information for business decisions
- *Analysts* Providing critical analysis skills in summarizing information
- *Consultants* Working with teams within the organization or with vendors
- *Communicators* To keep everyone apprised of available information and other services
- Web Masters To provide connectivity of internal and external information as a one-step process

These competencies allow the information specialists to work as partners with vendors and the company MIS unit in developing new information products. This is very important as more and more commercial and internal information migrate to the electronic information. It will be the role of information specialists to insure the integrity of the information that will be accessible by these products. Within the organization the information specialist can play a pivotal role in designing the content of both their home page and that of their organization. This will include the need to constantly monitor the content of these pages t to be sure that intellectual property rights are being violated. Additionally the information specialist can work with units within the organization to develop the organization's Intranet. This will include identifying and providing those information services needed by the entire company not just those at the organization's headquarters.

KNOWLEDGE MANAGERS

Others at this meeting are going to spend more time discussing the role of the Knowledge Manager, I just want to briefly acknowledge how this is a new and more comprehensive role that many Information Specialists will want to seek..

It is these new competencies discussed in the previous section which have allowed many information specialists to consolidate their new responsibilities and to become knowledge managers within their organizations. These knowledge managers coordinate information audits, are responsible for developing the organization's knowledge base, have put into place knowledge mapping as a means to integration information functions and have made the effort to be seen as full-fledged partners in the development and maintenance of the organization's Intranet. These knowledge managers have been able to successfully articulate to upper management the importance of these services to the overall profitability of the organization. In addition to the papers presented more information on the implications of knowledge management to the field as a whole has been documented in a videoconference cosponsored by Knight Ridder and the Special Libraries Association held this past October at several sites across the United States and Canada. A video of this conference entitled *Getting Out of the Box: The Knowledge Management Opportunity* by contacting the Special Libraries Association.

Several of our colleagues are featured in this video and show the full extent of what can be achieved by information specialists in this new competitive environment which is so dependent on an information to achieve an advantage over the competition. They have shown how important it is to manage change to achieve success.

SERVICE CHALLENGES

Sense of Community: The virtual organization provides many challenges. The first problem is developing a sense of community. Today it is possible to have people on the road, permanently stationed in another state or country or working from home. Creating a cohesive feeling of the mission of the organization and a feeling of camaraderie among members of a team regardless of where they work. It takes a commitment from upper management as well as immediate supervisors to achieve this sense of community. The information center can play a role by making sure that all members of the organization are kept regularly informed of their services and to regularly survey to determine if there are additional services that need to be provided.

Identifying Individual Needs: In a virtual organization where many of the employees are not in a central location, innovate means must be used to identify information needs. This includes the development a variety of products, conducting with follow ups to ascertain if the needed information was received and to conduct regular evaluation of all of these processes. A variety of methods must be considered from phone calls, mail, email and using the quick-cam on your computer to talk face to face. This helps to eliminate the feeling of remoteness from those who are not near the information center.

Cross-Cultural Communication: As your organization becomes more global, many of the new hires will be from other countries and different cultural views on how to seek information services. It will be your challenge to satisfying those information needs recognizing that you may need to find new ways of determining what they need to successfully complete their jobs.

The Work Day: It is possible within a virtual organization for you to have demand for information beyond your information center's normal service hours. Part of this can be handled from your home page which can provide directions for obtaining information; you can also identifying contract employees in other time zones that can provide immediate response to information queries and providing regular training for your users so they can do some information retrieval for themselves. All of this is in addition to doing standard information profiles and automatic delivery of relevant information to their personal computers.

Multiplicity of Information Resources: More people are developing new information resources and new information management software packages. It is also true that there is the opportunity for employees located at various sites within a virtual organization to want to purchase new information products. Purchasing decisions for this software and hardware products can not be decentralized. Information specialists will need to be on constant alert that acquisition of such products are discussed with them prior to installation so that accessibility on the organization's Intranet is not impeded. Monitoring and evaluating these new products must be a high priority item for the organization and for the information specialist.

Network Security: Network security is a high priority for all organizations. As more and more company planning documents are added to the Intranet, the possibility of competitive espionage increases. Network security will be a growth industry for some time to come. As information specialists we participate in the decision making as to the level of security to be sure that all employees have the needed accessibility to all the information they need to successfully do their jobs.

Archiving Concerns: Most systems producers blithely discuss the archiving functions of their systems. As we move further and further away from maintaining paper files, the integrity and accessibility of these archives become increasingly important. As information specialists we know how important older information can be to support current activities. There are also legal considerations. We read about investigations in to past corporate activities for possible fraud or investigation pension funds or personnel records. We have also read about old files which were stored in formats which can no longer be read by the new system. These concerns are real and need to be revisited at regular intervals and the records management policy needs to reflect this.

Intellectual Property Concerns: The virtual organization which relies on the Internet and the Intranet must also be concerned about not violating intellectual property rights. An international commission is currently trying to resolve the key issues involved in protecting everyone's intellectual property rights. A quick solution to this problem is not expected but it is an issue that needs to be revisited at regular intervals. The new electronic world has made it easier than before to quickly transfer information from a site and incorporate into your site. The information specialist will be one of the key people in monitoring the content the organization's home page. This role will be to monitor information content and to be sure the organization in compliance with any existing protocols. No organization wants to in the situation that EXXON found itself several years ago. This can become a bigger problem when your organization is operating in several countries where there may be other acceptable ways to do business. Information Specialists can help the organization to develop an ethics code.

Technostress: New software, new software enhancements, new information products, new improved information products, new hardware, new hardware improvements, new systems and system upgrades any and all of these contribute to the technostress that Information Specialists are feeling. There is no immediate hope that the number of new products or enhancements will slow down, but we need to become masters of the technology rather than letting it master us. It is very easy to just stop and wait for the perfect product to come along, yet many of us have grown comfortable with the concept of continuous improvement which must be acquired as we have learned from the marketers of fashion and automotive companies. Therefore decisions need to be made and accept the fact that a particular purchase was a good decision and implement it. Do not feel under pressure to immediately acquire an upgrade unless it has new features you need. This philosophy will help you to provide a more standardize access system for the organization to use in its virtual environment.

Information Overload: I have already referred to one type of information overload in the preceding paragraph, the other information overload is the easy availability of getting hundreds of "hits" when doing very simple information queries. We have developed search strategies to minimize the number of "hits". The Internet is being touted as everyone's information source, yet when many people use it , they are overwhelmed with the responses they receive as an answer to a question. Most people are not efficient information searchers and do not understand how to phrase questions to get relevant information. Since today's world is so competitive, it does not contribute to profitability for inexperienced searcher to do their own searching. Even if we train them, most information products are changing so fast that an effective search strategy for one month may not be as effective a month or two later. Providing effective information retrieval training to employees across the spectrum of a virtual organization is possible for basic information needs. Research queries and analysis should be done by information specialists. to minimize information overload for employees.

SOME NEW REALITIES

Constant change is here to stay and new coping skills must be mastered in order to deal with the changes. Some of these strategies can be crafted within the new teamwork environment that is being developed within organizations. For the virtual organization this state of constant change provides the greatest single challenge to remaining competitive. A very reliable communication process must be adopted to be sure that everyone has the opportunity to be kept inform of those matters that affect them.

Do not ignore those users who want to be able to satisfy their basic information needs. The mass media as a whole have been informing the world that all the information they need for any solution is only a few keystrokes away. Many of the new employees are more computer literate than older employees and have many basic skills which just need to be refreshed. The challenge here is to know which employees need or want particular type of information access training. The other challenge is keep employees aware that the world to information is a morass of both good and bad information; complete and incomplete information, reliable and unreliable information, and comprehensive and incomplete information resources. Unless they high information literacy skills they need to turn to you for assistance or guidance for relevant information. The virtual corporation provides a challenging environment in which to do this monitoring of employee's information skills.

As the virtual organization is seen as a normal way to conduct business, it is more important to provide a seamless, one step information access process to both internal and external information. This is why new network security systems need to be evaluated in terms of providing this type of access. It is this seamless approach which will help to build that sense of community and permit the employees to be very productive and efficient.

SUCCESS

To be successful you need to become a strategic partner in the organization's planning process. Those who want to become Knowledge Managers see this as a critical role. This aids you in becoming an agent of change and aiding the organization to put knowledge to work to maintain its competitive edge.

Working within a virtual organization provides many opportunities for you to employ all of the competencies which you bring to your position and allows you to develop new innovative ways to satisfy information needs of a clientele beyond the walls of your information center. This is no time to be bored or self-satisfied as a whole new world or challenges and opportunities exist for those working for a virtual organization. The new technology has made it possible for us to succeed at developing a variety of ways to satisfy a vast variety of information needs. Being seen as strategic information partners within our organizations is now a possibility for all of those who are willing to take up the challenges that this new virtual world offers us.

Joy M. Park
McKinsey & Company
November 1996

In keeping with our theme of **"The Virtual Workplace: One Size Doesn't Fit All"** , this paper examines two very different corporations, each of which is "virtual" in distinct ways, and the role played by their information centers have initiating, structuring or managing the organization's knowledge. Some of the characteristics which differentiate one virtual organization from another, such as the maturity of the organization, it's stability, culture, and the reasons the organization has assumed a virtual form, influence the scope and success of its knowledge management efforts.

Virtual businesses can be characterized by their position along a "virtual continuum". At one extreme of the continuum are highly virtual organizations characterized by low physical, temporal or bureaucratic boundaries. Their cohesiveness is based upon shared interests. Electronic/online communities belong at this end of the continuum. The form they take is shaped by the social needs of their members.

Further towards the center of the continuum are moderately virtual organizations. They take several forms; one form emerges when a corporation has to change from its traditional physical organization, bounded by geography, bureaucracy or technology. "Going virtual" provides a way for the organization to achieve change. Transcendent virtual organizations evolve after a traditional physical organization has lost its strength. Virtual workgroups form which cut across the established hierarchy, transcending physical/political boundaries. This model is common where re-engineering, TQM, or other cross-functional teams have formed.

Another, opportunistic form may emerge when a virtual corporation appears to be a single corporate entity, although it is actually comprised of numerous legally/geographically separate entities. When each individual component leverages its individual strengths into strong business system, it achieves its goal: conserved resources, and high returns within a short time-frame.

Hybrid organizations selectively utilize both the traditional local organizational forms and leverage virtual strengths. Shared culture (values, language, behavior) permeates the hybrid organization, giving it enduring strength.

The following observations are based on a decade's work experiences, as an information professional in two very different organizations. They represent my personal opinions only.   Both organizations possess characteristics of virtual organizations:- McKinsey through both its worldwide presence through offices and its deeply embedded Practice communities which span the globe; MCI through its physically dispersed presence throughout the United States, its fundamental shift of focus from function to a customer, and a technologically "wired" culture which favors electronic forms of communication. Both organizations' information professionals regard the management of external and internal knowledge as a crucial aspect of their service; McKinsey's corporate philosophy regarding the high value of internal knowledge has resulted in an excellent knowledge management infrastructure, which incorporates, but reaches far beyond the information centers; MCI's approach to knowledge management has been largely driven by the Information centers, and is in its early stages of development.

MCI as a Virtual Organization

MCI can be described as both opportunistic and transcendent in its virtuality.

It is opportunist in its preference for acquiring needed skill sets, new businesses and products, through partnering or direct acquisition rather than growing these capabilities in-house. Short-term relationships with vendors, contractors, partners are the norm. The Email culture of this technologically "wired" organization is pervasive, circumventing normal human work/rest cycles, and attracting high-energy employees, able to take advantage of opportunities in the marketplace which allow neither the luxuries of lead-time nor reflection. MCI describes itself as having a "Cowboy culture" -- rules are to be questioned; technology is to be pushed to its limits; products must get to market fast. it. MCI's Human Resources policy supports an open door policy, which permits an employee to go over the head of a supervisor when ever there is good reason. Yet another characteristic of a company that breaks down bureaucratic barriers, and is willing to risk losing formality if the prize is freedom and speed.

Several divisions within MCI could be described as a transcendent virtual organizations. The Systems Engineering Division typified this form. Re-engineering forced teams within business units to shift from a geographically-defined focus, where members of the teams were predominantly all systems engineers, to a customer-defined focus (a customer who was physically thousands of miles away, and a marketing or other business professional).New skills were needed to communicate with different professions and cultures, and new technologies were needed to speed development of new products through geographically separated processes. In addition, the whole corporation was constantly undergoing re-organizations and downsizings. Employees had to transcend the old reporting relationships and patterns of collaboration and assume new ones under a virtual organization.

These circumstances have a negative impact on the organization's retention of knowledge. Systems Engineering is a knowledge-intensive profession, and the potential for "corporate Alzheimer's" in both the administrative and engineering functions under these conditions is high.

Within this macro environment, MCI's three Information Resource Centers existed, each philosophically and physically distant from the other. Both within the IRCs and the corporation as a whole, huge funding discontinuities occurred month to month, unit to unit. Uneven technology infrastructure, and equally uneven investment in external knowledge presented challenges that threatened the organization's shared knowledge base.

In a series of moves over a five year span, the three Information Resource Centers forged a working plan that was successful in solving the most critical problems in corporate-wide information infrastructure. They segmented their customers, identified the highest value services and products customers needed, then devised strategies for delivering them. They created common work processes, common work tools, and made a commitment to a joint vision of a virtual library which would serve the information and research needs of the corporation.(1)

The IRCs have achieved success in joint procurement for external information, creation of internal knowledge repositories (for technical documentation, as well as for many corporate support functions), they have identified and made freely available "core" information, and have played a critical role in being early adopters of workgroup and work-sharing technologies.

Currently, the networkMCI Library (nML) is one virtual organization, drawing on staff from Texas, Colorado and Washington, D.C. It has assumed the role of "Mouthpiece" of the corporation, and its electronic presence is the gathering place for its thousands of internal virtual customers. One of the earliest adopters and experimenters with the Internet, it has developed over 2200 Intranet Web Pages, and 22 external Internet pages.

. nML is also a model of successful electronic information procurement, having played an important role in influencing vendors to take the Lotus Notes or Internet distribution channel, and having forged models of pricing and packaging that have now become an industry norm. Their "virtual" success is partly a function of the industry in which they reside, partly a function of the special mix of mentors and professionals who comprise the Information Center community, - and partly because they are unafraid to innovate and take a risk.

"Knowledge Management" within this corporate context, includes the selection, retention, and dissemination of both internal information, and externally published news, information and research. Both information streams integrated into a unified front -end that can be accessed at the desk-top by the greater corporate community. Exciting developments in defining "experts", and taking a leadership role in facilitating the growth of knowledge around areas of expertise may be the next steps the IRCs can take, as this function is still in its infancy within the corporation.

McKinsey's Learning Organization

A very different kind of success in managing knowledge within a virtual corporation is found at McKinsey and Company. McKinsey is a worldwide management consulting firm; it is organized into both local offices and into global practices which are virtual. For this reason, it can be called a hybrid virtual organization.

Although each office (located in 35 countries, with almost double that number of offices) reflects management practices of its own country, all share a common philosophy, draw on a common base of experience and skills, and adhere to a common set of standards with respect to professional responsibility, quality of work, caliber of staff, and problem solving approaches.

McKinsey's consulting teams work with clients, and draw upon leadership from two sources: at a local level a senior manager guides the team; in a virtual context, the team utilizes the Firm's in-depth functional and industry knowledge through structured "communities of practice", which are called "Centers of Competence" .

These Centers of Competence were developed in the early 1980s   The many practice groups each focus on a particular management function or issue (marketing, corporate finance, operational effectiveness, as well as many others.) The center's job is to develop new approaches to services, disseminate ideas through publications, databases, conferences, and networks of people.(5)

Clientele Development Sectors, which focus on an industry (for example, automotive, health-care) were also developed. These practice groups share a similar charge to build knowledge and disseminate it throughout the organization.

A third kind of community in the knowledge structure are Special Initiatives or working groups which re-integrate and synthesize at the highest levels, the knowledge of the Centers and Sectors.

Although a decade earlier the firm had been building an internal knowledge base, this tri-part structure marked the beginning of a new level of commitment to knowledge building within the Firm. (2) McKinsey's commitment to continuous intellectual renewal was evident in these remarks from Fred Gluck, the Managing Director of the Firm in the early 1980s:

"Unless we take conscious steps to synthesize and re-synthesize our points of view and beliefs about key areas of our practice and ensure that they are internalized by a significant portion of the consulting staff, we will lose our professional leadership and simply become purveyors of conventional wisdom"."

In this knowledge-rich, structured context of the Firm, Research & Information Centers (R&Is) are integrated into both the local and virtual communities of practice. Professional information specialists pursue either generalist (offering broad research support) or specialist careers (offering deep, industry or practice-specific support). They work with both external and internal resources, and begin their research support for consultants at a high level of shared understanding.

One of the critical tools of knowledge sharing is the common language (Thesaurus) and frameworks/analytical models which are used across the Firm. Information professional's work is often integrated into client teams, and are evaluated based on the value their work has brought to the team. An ethic of sharing across all R&Is around the world has been developed (as well, of course, as carefully defined "firewalls" to ensure confidentiality is maintained).

Adoption of Lotus Notes, Intranets, and other technologies are planned, criteria including robustness and reliability. Intelligent tradeoffs are made between customization at the local level and economies of effort through conforming to a centrally administered model.

McKinsey's resources cover both internal and external information. Two of many important internal resources are two online databases , one of which contains client experience, the other containing sanitized, practice or functional knowledge crystallized from McKinsey's global learnings.

These resources transcend mere archives of internal information through special efforts to articulate lessons learned from each engagement and to identify knowledge gaps in a timely manner. These, and many other specialized internal databases, are supplemented by hotlines and "First Alerts" which provide graduated levels of access and linkages to experts and those seeking expertise.

McKinsey's Knowledge Management infrastructure has been developed over many years, and its form is an outcome of the corporate culture and the organization's values rather than a recent response to worksharing technology. It has depth of coverage and functionality of structure that represents a core asset.

What next?

The literature regarding Knowledge Management comes from a variety of professions, some from the IRM (Information and Records Management)community who stress archiving an organization's recorded information; some from EIS (Executive Information Systems) or IT (Information Technology) communities, who focus on utilizing client-server architecture and workgroup software to bring external and internal information into a unified, desktop environment. With reengineering, new emphasis has been given to its function in gathering metrics, and streamlining processes. Librarians recognize the strategic role their function plays in the growth of their organization's knowledge, and advocate the facilitation and synthesis of these various approaches.

Brook Manville and Nathaniel Foote, leaders in the field have said: "*Knowledge Management, a hot buzz phrase in executive circles, implies a systematic process for assembling and controlling this nebulous resource, just as companies now control inventory, raw materials, and other physical resources. But Knowledge Management also implies controlling people. And that is destined to fail...Organizations need a new approach...One that takes them beyond Knowledge Management. Call it post-modern reengineering. This approach views an organization as a human community whose collective wisdom represents a distinctive edge against competitors...*" (3)

Manville's and Foote's conception of corporate Knowledge Management embrace all aspects of the field, IRM, IT, Information Specialist's as well as that of organizational design and strategic management.   Their   emphasis on the human side is distinctive:

"Collective knowledge that moves the needle in achieving world class performance is based on the skills and experience of people who do the work...These informal networks have been called the "community of practice"... A group of professionals, informally bound together through exposure to a common class of problems, common pursuit of solutions, and thereby themselves embodying a store of knowledge..."

What is also distinctive is the emphasis they put on moving the state of the art beyond the definitions we are commonly using for Knowledge Management. They map a path to advance beyond simply providing communications, beyond simply communicating what is already in a recorded format, beyond collecting and disseminating, and beyond the traditional focus on transactions and automation. Rather they offer three fundamental principles:

"1. …Communities of practice form and share knowledge on the basis of pull by individual members, not a centralized push of information. Knowledge based strategies must not focus on collecting and disseminating information but rather on creating a mechanism for practitioners to reach out to other practitioners.
Business managers must set high performance aspirations and then create incentives and systems for practitioners to solve problems together. IS managers must then develop systems that facilitate an exchange of ideas and solutions, as well as track participation.

"2. Knowledge based communities focused on communities of practice must be linked to performance and ought to be linked to measurable by traditional and widely understood business metrics. The communities of practice must be able to see the link between their sharing and hard business outcomes appreciated by senior management…

"3. Communities of practice must have the necessary tools to form, evolve and develop as freely as possible. The paradigm shift here is the IS department's surrender of "doing for the user". The more practitioners feel that they have to get in the queue for some technical specialist to build what they need, the greater the barrier to community formation."

"Growing knowledge rather than simply managing it" is an expression Manville and Foote use, which I believe sums up a goal we can envision as we continually redefine our mission as information professionals in this increasingly virtual world.

References:

1. Kimberly Allen's and Mary Ellen Bates' excellent articles in numerous online publications describe in more detail some of the Lotus Notes initiatives undertaken at MCI. Helen Gordon, Larry Enoch, and David Tinsley in Richardson Texas and Colorado Springs Colorado were also important visionaries and architects of MCI's "Virtual Library" initiatives.

2. Several consulting firms' knowledge management efforts are described in two excellent articles by Thomas A. Stewart "Mapping Corporate Brainpower" in **Fortune**, v.132, n.9, p.209 ff, October 30, 1995; and "The Invisible Key to Success" in **Fortune**, v.134, n.3, p.173 ff, August 5, 1996.

2. Brook Manville and Nathaniel Foote, "Harvest Your Workers' Knowledge" in **Datamation**, v. 42, n.13, p78 ff., July 1996.

REAL PEOPLE ---- VIRTUAL ORGANIZATIONS

Telework- the practice of working or managing work remotely from the office, customer, or work source on a regular, structured basis. Flexiwork - the practice of offering any form of flexibility in work organization including telework plus 'hoteling' or similarly flexible offices, virtual organizations.

Even the quickest review of the literature on telecommuting, remote work centers, nomadic workers, flexiwork, and virtual organizations leads you into a thicket of contradictions, anecdotal evidence, and wildly diverse data. Dredging through these leads to the realization that there is a confusion in terms as well as writers' bias based on personal philosophy. Almost all concentrate on knowledge work, as we will here. Some see forms of telework as the future and others see flexiwork ideas already becoming obsolete as the nature of work changes.

Telework's advantages include:	And, disadvantages include:
Attract employees from more sources, such as disabled or remote areas.	Exploit people in low wage areas
	Pay for piecework only
Employees see as a benefit	'Independent contractor' vs jobs
Employee retention	Company security issues
Energy savings	Company privacy issues
Environmental benefits	Individual privacy issues
Family-friendly aspects	Socially isolated, alienated workers
Improved customer service	Loss of creativity in isolation
Reduced office costs	Work expands into other areas of life
Can reduce stress of commuting, work interruptions	Work hours spread into all 24 hours

When you look at actual telework/flexiwork practices, you discover another wealth of contradictions. Nearly three-fourths of all large US companies indicate they offer some form of flexible workplace. Many studies indicate smaller organizations are the biggest users. Yet, less than 2% of US workers actually work on a flexiwork basis. Organizations such as Pacific Bell and Coopers and Lybrand brag that they have 4-6% of their employees in some form of telework and use this as a recruiting and retention tool. And, despite all the stated promises of telecommuting which often assume it is full-time, surveys show most employees telecommute only 1-2 days a week and only for 6 to 18 months. The Smart Valley Initiative studies deem telecommuting as still being in the 'early adoption phase' despite over 20 years of experience in flexiwork. Companies which have higher participation rates are usually those with an internal champion who has pushed the organization. In countries where governments which have supported telework efforts extensively, as many European countries have, rates of 5-7% workforce participation are being experienced.

And now some business theorists and organization scientists are moving on to the concepts of the networked economy and the digital economy. They posit a radical change in the nature of organizations as we currently know them. And, in turn, a move beyond working in the same old organizations with only an overlay of telework or flexiwork as a cost saving measure. These ideas see the office as a system, not a place, and work roles changing into networks or other new relationships.

Let us look first at telework/flexiwork. Flexiwork options are currently possible for many people in many organizations. Thus, flexiwork is an option more of us could work in and with now. There are two critical aspects of any form of flexiwork: people and information. One advantage of the traditional office was the collocation of people of differing skills and knowledge with those who directed the work and with the resources to do the work. Work could be easily directed or redirected as needed and information was relatively readily available. Informal communications and information flows provided support and timely work goal adjustments. Trust developed among workers as daily relationships grew. With flexiwork, organizations face critical issues and concerns about people and information that either do not exist or, more commonly, are not recognized as so critical within a traditional office.

Despite the yawning divides in theories and in practices, there is relative agreement on the compelling reasons for organizations to implement flexiwork plans. Today, most organizations believe they must focus on customer satisfaction and cost reduction. This demands in-depth knowledge of the marketplace, an ability to create products or services which exceed customers' expectations, and superb customer service; all tied up with a cost-effective bow.

Flexiwork offers a range of benefits which can help achieve these goals. These include:
- closeness to the market-makers for advance information on new concepts or issues
- closeness to the customers to provide quicker, more responsive service
- extended hours of customer service
- extended hours of work within each 24 hour period
- ability to recruit and retain the best 'high performance' employees
- ability to withstand disasters, such as fires, terrorist actions, or natural catastrophes
- cost savings through reduced office space and travel.

However, organizations face several challenges to obtaining these benefits. These include:
- information must be able to be shared rapidly and easily all across the organization and its employees
- information must be able to be used anywhere
- the underlying culture must support flexiwork's requirements for effective information flow and for management by results
- management must be trained in remote management and must practice flexiwork options.

▸ trust becomes an increasingly critical element in employee relationships.

Earlier I noted the wide disparity between existing flexiwork programs and their actual use. Organizations have many models of mobile work already, especially in sales and field rep staffs. Yet, when it comes to flexiwork, many organizations still see this as a special privilege to be granted to a favored employee or to assist a valued employee with a temporary family or medical problem. Managers and those who are still required to be there every day wonder if the person is really working or feel aggrieved at picking up perceived slack. Even in more open operations, flexiwork is often not available to the majority or even not available to everyone in the same type of position. Employees also fear a loss of effectiveness as they are cut off from information sources and a loss of promotion or career-enhancing opportunities from a lack of 'face time'. These are the most common reasons why so few people actually work in a flexiwork situation despite the buzz.

Conversely, some organizations have moved from flexiwork as an employee option to a mandated way of working. Employees are forced out of traditional offices into working at home, in a virtual office, or into hoteling as the organization restructures, reengineers, downsizes or whatever. The success of such mandated change requires management training, effective systems to support the changes, a realization that a change in one part of the system creates others, and employee comfort levels with the new ways of working. Such changes can succeed where vision, communication and involvement are present and effective. Failure is depressingly common.

Worse yet, in both voluntary and mandated flexiwork efforts, many organizations have not significantly changed work processes. Thus, flexiwork programs usually produce one-time productivity increases or cost reductions but seldom produce on-going or long-term productivity gains.

An organization considering flexiwork needs to look at it as an integral part of the overall strategy. Flexiwork must be chosen as a way to operate because it directly supports organization strategy and the achievement of important goals. From this perspective, the organization can then develop the forms which meet its needs. Flexiwork requires that organizational structures, work processes, information flow, and job design all be built to support it to have an effective, successful program. The organizational design issues do not simply support a flexiwork plan. Many of them also, if well-designed, will improve the effectiveness of the total organization rather than be special to the flexiwork employees. Dr. Sims of Cornell University in a 1996 IFMA study titled "Managing the Reinvented Workplace" identifies nine keys to success in flexiwork efforts. The very first is that top management must look at flexiwork as a major investment and a major change in the way the organization works which it must support and sustain over time.

It may be that it is the recognition of the need to review and revise the organization's structures and behaviors that is what keeps flexiwork efforts small. The real and hard work of linking organizational strategy to daily activities is given more lip service than elbow grease.

Most studies indicate managers are the biggest, if not the only, problem in flexiwork. Managers are accused of resisting the loss of presence on a daily basis and of unwillingness to do the planning inherent in working with people in multiple locations. Yet, most organizations do not have the processes or structure in place to manage flexiwork effectively. Managers are not trained on communications skills or performance planning and management. Compensation systems call for merit pay yet reward employees for time worked and willingness to do work that is often not important to organizational goals. Availability of information is chaotic and localized rather than open and multi-channel. Communications and systems - computer, telecommunications, and others - may not effectively support people outside the major locations. Risk avoidance may be more important than risk identification and management. In larger organizations, the flexiwork procedures are often quite detailed and telecommuting employee contracts spell out everything in great detail. The burdensome aspects and approval process create many hurdles. In all these situations, a manager would be a fool to encourage flexiwork options since they could undercut unit success.

Organizations which see a use or need for flexiwork as a part of their strategy must evaluate their entire organization carefully to design effective systems. This review includes:
- the organization's culture and any underlying cultural difficulties,
- the tasks which the organization wishes to do,
- organizational structures and work processes,
- information needs and flow,
- communications needs and flow,
- work flow, work design and job design,
- technical support and training needed for flexiwork,
- hidden costs in keep employees feeling connected, and
- technology and its impact on the organization.

Organizational structures are under significant attack as global competition and technological change influence almost all organizations. While large organizations have a strong influence on the perspective and ideas which people accept, no single organizational concept has arisen to replace the hierarchy model. It remains one of the most effective ways for a small number of people to coordinate large scale, complex tasks. However, hierarchies do not recognize, adopt or adapt to new concepts well so other forms of organization are being tried. This hierarchical model is probably one reason flexiwork has remained a minor reality.

Additionally, traditional ways of working provide significant benefits to many. Informal relationships provide support and assistance for employees to do their work. Individuals learn who they can trust through direct observation. Informal interactions may enhance creativity and innovation. Individuals who are interested in the process or who are energized by others thrive in these environments. Many people develop friends through their workplace. It may be the source of organization for leisure activities. The new worker fresh from schooling learns work habits, tolerance, and how to be a team worker. Organizations thrive by creating a sense of belonging which meets deep human needs to belong. And, for many, the office remains a source of status and recognition. For some, it also provides respite from personal problems.

New forms of organizational structure are appearing - and disappearing - across a wide range of organizations. Structured as teams, spider webs, changing coalitions, symphony orchestra or basketball team, the issues of flexiwork in an organization remain much the same.

Managers need to be trained in effective communications and performance management techniques in any organization but this is far more critical when trying to make flexiwork viable. Further, they should experience flexiwork themselves enough so that they understand and make the changes it requires.
There really are no secrets to management success in flexiwork - they are the same practices and efforts good managers use anywhere. Managers who wish to support flexiwork need good project management skills. They must learn how to communicate precisely and to consistently follow up oral communications with summaries or notes via some other channel. Flexiwork is easiest to implement for positions with the following characteristics:
- ▸ discrete tasks or projects are common
- ▸ major work requirements can easily be scheduled in advance or anticipated
- ▸ results are specific deliverables or measurable
- ▸ work includes information or documents which can be transmitted electronically, or
- ▸ there is a substantial telephone communications component.

Individuals who are interested in flexiwork options should look at their situation carefully to evaluate it and to present a 'business plan" to management. This includes considering:
- ▸ organizational culture and responsiveness
- ▸ defining the work tasks and interactions with others
- ▸ evaluating the work processes and flow and any changes which would be potentially advantageous or harmful
- ▸ assessing technology needs and problems
- ▸ defining expectations, including what the organization needs to provide
- ▸ establishing communications process and feedback loops
- ▸ building in a schedule and evaluation plans

Individuals also need to assess their own abilities. Excellent organizational and communications skills are needed. The ability to separate work from the rest of life and to enforce that with others is vital for those who work at home. In many cases, the ability to develop and project a strongly competent persona remotely is also important.

Managers and employees interested in flexiwork need to address what work is appropriately done in such options and how other work will be done. Managers need to assess the individual's ability to work effectively in a flexiwork plan. Some organizations hire for this while others only allow longer service, highly productive, self motivated employees to be in such programs. Work plans and performance management must be based on defined objectives and standards. Most successful flexiwork and virtual organizations run on multi-channel communications with lots of individual attention including regularly scheduled face-to-face meetings. Such organizations also recognize the importance of events with strong socializing components as a way to develop relationships and trust with people one teleworks with. Organizational concerns must be addressed including: legal issues such as employment, safety, and zoning laws; liability and workers compensation insurance; remote access and systems security.

Having discussed some of the issues of flexiwork in existing organizations, I would like to turn to what some organizational theories see as the paradigm shift we are currently entering - the digital or networked economy. Many of us do not think of our work in a networked context, yet we actually do some portion of our work that way. The ideas of the digital/networked economy are based on the increasing convergence of communications, computing, and content. This convergence has already been relatively visible in scientific research and education delivery. It is increasingly changing the way we do business and the nature of the organization.
Proponents see a revolution as organizations are TRANSFORMED to compete effectively in a global marketplace. This transformation, enabled by information technologies, will allow high levels of customer service and responsiveness and innovation. Organizational learning and agility will be the key success factors.

The network as organization structure is similar to the network as computing technology. While all members of the network will share a purpose and common views or goals, there is independence. Members must be able to achieve on their own and to benefit from the network. Links are multiple and extensive. Those members who bring unique perspectives and abilities emerge as leaders. The process of developing the common goals and focus becomes a vital part of the way to accomplish them as well as a way to develop trust among the group members. Such a networked organizational structure assumes flexiwork rather than adds it on to an existing organization. While it also sees people and information as the critical keys to success in transforming the organization to meet future challenges, it focuses more on value added than on cost savings benefits of 'traditional' telework advocates.

In a digital/networked economy, success depends on an intense collaboration of knowledge workers within an organization. Organizations must provide their members with the ability to share information rapidly and easily so that it can be used anywhere. They must be able to recognize and use all the knowledge within the organization and provide a climate which makes on-going learning the norm. Developing relationships and trust is key in these organization structures also. This presents organizations with a need for some mutuality -something to offer the member in return for trust.

The changing nature of work in a digital/networked economy presents many new opportunities and challenges. Few organizations are prepared for these. What happens as the workforce becomes distributed across geographic, cultural and time barriers? How will organizations plan for and cope with the demands for open systems in all areas so as to minimize the disruptions of technology changes or power/system outages? How will organizations create conditions conducive to "trust" among employees? If successful organizations must address life-long learning and retraining and the quality of worklife, how will they do so? If we are already seeing negative health effects from current levels of multitasking, what is likely to happen in more complex interconnections? As career paths change from a restricted access highway with regular interchanges to other highways into rambling footpaths through the mountains, how do organizations assist individuals in the trek?

Organizations and individuals have attitudes, cultures, and ways of working that are often maintained without conscious thought. If the virtual organization in the digital economy is truly based on "mass customization" of products and services with the treatment of each customer in a highly responsive and individualized way, then how do we get there? If you and your organization wish to change, the hard work begins in a most traditional way. You must create a vision of the future and one of the current reality. From these two, you can create a gap analysis and design a plan to move to the new vision. And then you will have to continually recheck and adjust your course as the vision changes as the world changes.

Patricia A. Frame
Strategies for Human Resources
703 751-2832
email: StratHR4PF@aol.com

SUGGESTED RESOURCES for HUMAN RESOURCE ISSUES

1. Internet sites for telecommuting and telework information:

* GTE's Telecommuting Guide: http://wcn.gte.com/telecommuting
* Pacific Bell's Telecommuting Guide: http://www.pacbell.com/Lib/TCGuide
* European resources: http://www.eto.org.uk/faq/faq03.html
* BT's Teleworking Training Guide:
http://btlabs1.labs.bt.com/innovate/telework/reports/index.htm

2. Non-profit association dedicated to promoting telecommuting:

Telecommuting Advisory Council
204 E St. N.E.
Washington, D.C. 20002
phone: 202 547-6157   Internet: http://www.telecommute.org
There are also local chapters in several areas.

3. Books

Digital Harmony by Arno Penzias. HarperBusiness paperback

The Age of the Network by Jessica Lipnack & Jeffrey Stamps.   omneo

Business Wisdom of the Electronic Elite by Geoffrey James. Times Business

The Digital Economy by Don Tapscott. McGraw Hill

COMPETENCIES
for
SPECIAL
LIBRARIANS
of the
21*st* CENTURY

Submitted to the SLA Board of Directors
by the Special Committee on Competencies for Special Librarians
Joanne Marshall, Chair; Bill Fisher; Lynda Moulton; and Roberta Piccoli

May 1996

Competencies for Special Librarians of the 21st Century

FULL REPORT

May 1996

Background to the Document

The Special Libraries Association (SLA), an organization of dynamic and change-oriented information professionals, has long been interested in the knowledge requirements of new entrants to the field. The Association's members have explored and shared their vision of the Competencies and skills required for special librarianship in many forums over the years as shown by the accompanying bibliography. This document is an attempt to synthesize and build upon this earlier work in the light of the rapid social, technological and workplace transformations that are taking place.

Competencies have been defined as the interplay of knowledge, understanding, skills and attitudes required to do a job effectively from the point of view of both the performer and the observer (Murphy, 1991). *The unique competencies of the special librarian include in-depth knowledge of print and electronic information resources in specialized subject areas and the design and management of information services that meet the strategic information needs of the individual or group being served.*

In personal career development terms, competencies can also be thought of as flexible knowledge and skills that allow the special librarian to function in a variety of environments and to produce a continuum of value-added, customized information services that cannot be easily duplicated by others. At a time when professionals in all fields are being encouraged to invest in themselves and to prepare for employment as independent contractors, it is critical that special librarians define their unique competencies and that they continue to improve the range of professional and personal competencies that will form the basis for their future careers.

The Audience

The primary audience for previous SLA documents on competencies has been library and information studies (LIS) educators. The need for communication between professional groups such as SLA and LIS educators is supported in the American Library Association (1992) guidelines for the accreditation of Masters' programs in library and information studies. Such communication can foster the development of curricula that respond to the needs and demands of the real world of information work. There is also a wider audience for this document. *Prospective students* who are considering special librarianship as a career can use this document as a guide to the content and approaches that they should look for in a LIS curriculum. As proactive lifelong learners, *currently practicing special librarians* will also find the competencies useful as a framework for defining their own professional development and continuing education needs.

Last, and of key importance, *managers who are responsible for hiring library and information professionals* as full-time employees, contract employees or as information brokers can use this document to inform themselves about the knowledge and skills of special librarians and the value that they add to the organization or to the particular task at hand.

The Environment

As we move towards the millennium, library and information professionals are facing at least three major paradigm shifts.

☐ The first shift is the *transition from paper to electronic media* as the dominant form of information storage and retrieval. Linked to this transition is the convergence of previously separate media, such as text, graphics, and sound, into multimedia resources.

☐ The second shift relates to the *increasing demand for accountability*, including a focus on customers, performance measurement, bench marking and continuous improvement. All of this is taking place in an era when the financial resources available for providing library and information services are shrinking.

☐ The third shift comes from *new forms of work organization* such as end-user computing, work teams, management delayering, job sharing, telework, outsourcing, downsizing and re-engineering.

All three of these shifts are related to a combination of factors such as global competition, new computing and communications technologies, and the perceived need to measure the productivity of knowledge and service workers.

We are facing these paradigm shifts at a time when the workforce is aging and when we as a profession are aging. In the year 2000, the average age of the worker in the United States will be 39 and this will increase until the last of the baby boom generation has reached retirement age in 2031 (Johnston and Packer, 1987, p.81). In an earlier era, we might have looked for innovation and change to come from increasing numbers of new entrants to the field of special librarianship; however, the demographics and the current economic situation have determined that those of us who are currently in the field must continue to play a vital and active role. This is why this document on competencies is addressed to both new entrants and practicing special librarians -- we must all learn and change together if we are to reach our full potential as information professionals in the information age. We must also communicate the broad range of competencies held by special librarians to current and prospective employers.

The changing landscape suggests that a document on competencies of special librarians produced in 1996 will necessarily take a different shape from those produced in earlier times when resources were more plentiful and change was proceeding at a slower pace. A document produced by SLA must also take into account the particular environments in which special librarians work. There are close to 15,000 members of SLA and almost 60% are employed in small libraries with six or fewer staff. Solo librarians are estimated to make up 30% to 50% of the membership and over half of the members work in corporate business settings. Increasing numbers of librarians are working as independent information brokers or in contract positions. In comparison to their colleagues in academic and public libraries, special librarians frequently work in settings without professional peers. As a result, special librarians must often work harder than librarians in other settings to make themselves recognizable and to align themselves with the strategic direction of the organization. Just as organizations are refocusing on their core competencies in response to global competition, it is time for special librarians to take a fresh look at what they do best and to reaffirm their commitment to continuing competence and growth.

The Value of the Special Librarian

The special librarian adds value by providing efficient and effective information services for a defined group of customers. The special librarian may be a full-time member of an information management team in an organization or hired on a part-time or contract basis for special projects. The unique contributions of the special librarian include expertise in the content and selection of the best available print and electronic information resources as well as a commitment to putting knowledge to work or, in other words, linking the information user with the right information resource at the right time.

The special librarian understands the critical role that information plays for organizations and for individuals and takes a holistic view of information needs and uses and the contexts in which they occur. The special librarian identifies, retrieves, organizes, repackages and presents information in an actionable form so that the potential for goal attainment is maximized. The special librarian helps control the flood of available information by selecting what is relevant and usable and, when required, analysing or synthesizing the content.

The special librarian is a technology application leader who works with other members of the information management team to design and evaluate systems for information access that meet user needs. Where required, the special librarian provides instruction and support so that end users can make optimal use of the information resources available to them. The special librarian is capable of working in the hybrid world of print and electronic media and providing the best mix of information resources in the most appropriate formats for the environment.

The special librarian plays a key role in developing information policy for the organization ensuring that access to all information resources -- from internal records to external databases -- is provided in the most strategically-effective and cost-effective manner. The special librarian also plays another important role in ensuring that contractual, legal and ethical obligations regarding information use are met. The electronic information age provides new opportunities for organizations to produce as well as use information products. Special librarians, given their familiarity with the information marketplace, can be key contributors to the development, marketing and use of information products.

Special librarians are knowledge-based practitioners who use research as a foundation for their own professional practice and who support the conduct of research through their professional associations such as SLA. Research has shown that the provision of appropriate information can lead to: better-informed decision-making; the ability to proceed to the next step in a project or task; improved relations with a client; and the exploitation of new business opportunities. The right information at the right time can also benefit the organization by saving the time of highly paid employees, avoiding poor business decisions, and even direct loss of funds (Marshall, 1993).

In the information age, special librarians are essential -- by responding with a sense of urgency to critical information needs they provide the information edge for the knowledge-based organization. In order to fulfill this key information role, special librarians require two main types of competencies:

> *Professional competencies* relate to the special librarian's knowledge in the areas of information resources, information access, technology, management and research and the ability to use these areas of knowledge as a basis for providing library and information services.

> *Personal competencies* represent a set of skills, attitudes and values that enable librarians to work efficiently; be good communicators; focus on continuing learning throughout their careers; demonstrate the value-added nature of their contributions; and survive in the new world of work.

The following sections highlight the major professional and personal competencies of special librarians and provide practical examples of the multitude of roles and tasks that special librarians can perform.

1.   Professional Competencies

The special librarian...

1.1   has expert knowledge of the content of information resources, including the ability to critically evaluate and filter them.

Practical examples: Evaluates print, CD-ROM and online versions of databases. Knows "the best" textbooks, journals and electronic resources in specific areas such as biology, marketing or accounting. Evaluates and selects key information resources, print and electronic, for a small research center. Sets up a desktop news wire service for a petrochemical company. Controls the over supply of information by selecting what is relevant and usable for the customer. Uses strategic thinking to perform information selection and analysis that meets specific organizational goals.

1.2   has specialized subject knowledge appropriate to the business of the organization or client.

Practical examples: In addition to their Masters degree in library and information studies, many special librarians have subject degrees at the undergraduate and postgraduate levels. Librarians frequently take additional courses in finance, management or other subjects related to their host organization. Maintains a view of the organization's business by reading core journals and other key sources. This enables the development of in-depth, subject specialty information services, including current awareness.

1.3   develops and manages convenient, accessible and cost-effective information services that are aligned with the strategic directions of the organization.

Practical examples: Develops a strategic plan linked to the business goals of the organization. Sets up effective management, supervision and budget processes. Builds an effective staff team to manage information services. Conducts intermediary searches for complex, difficult or multifoil searches. Obtains documents in print or electronic form. Builds a core in-house library collection. Analyzes and synthesizes information as required. Develops specialized thesauri and lists of indexing terms for databases.

1.4   provides excellent instruction and support for library and information service users.

Practical examples: Teaches Internet courses for employees. develops specialized end user searching courses on information resources related to current business goals. Keeps up-to-date with latest training and instructional techniques. Provides trouble-shooting service for employees who are accessing information services from the desktop. Provides online reference and assistance.

1.5   assesses information needs and designs and markets value-added information services and products to meet identified needs.

Practical examples: Conducts regular needs assessments using research tools such as questionnaires, focus groups and key informant interviews. Reports the results to management and demonstrates the relationship between needs and services provided. Identifies and meets information needs by becoming a member of project teams. Contributes unique or unusual needs assessment findings to the professional literature.

1.6   uses appropriate information technology to acquire, organize and disseminate

information.

Practical examples: Creates an online catalog of the library collection. Links catalog searching to a document delivery service. Works with the information management team to select appropriate software and hardware for desktop access to the library catalog and other databases. Provides a support service for electronic information service users. Keeps up-to-date with new electronic information products and modes of information delivery.

1.7   uses appropriate business and management approaches in to communicate the importance of information services to senior management.

Practical examples: Develops a business plan for the library. Calculates a return on investment for the library and its services. Develops a marketing plan for the library. Conducts a bench marking study. Reports to management on continuous quality improvement efforts. Demonstrates how library and information services add value to the organization. Acts as a resource for the organization on quality management, including ISO 9000 certification.

1.8   develops specialized information products for use inside or outside the organization or by individual clients.

Practical examples: Creates databases of in-house documents such as reports, technical manuals or resource materials used for special projects. Creates searchable full-text document files. Mounts online technical manuals created in-house. Creates a home page on the World Wide Web for the organization. Links the home page to other sites of interest on the Internet. Participates in knowledge management activities that create, capture, exchange, use and communicate the organization's "intellectual capital" (Remeikis, 1996).

1.9   evaluates the outcomes of information use and conducts research related to the solution of information management problems.

Practical examples: Gathers data related to needs assessment, program planning and evaluation. Develops measures of frequency of use of services, customer satisfaction and impact of information on organizational decision-making. Actively seeks opportunities for improvement and strives to be the best-in-class on key services such as current awareness, reference and resource sharing. Participates in research projects.

1.10   continually improves information services in response to the changing needs.

Practical examples: Monitors industry trends and disseminates information to key people in the organization or to individual clients. Refocuses information services on new business needs. Uses just-in-time document delivery to retain maximum flexibility. Monitors purchases of information products by departments to ensure that they are cost effective and aligned with current business needs.

1.11 is an effective member of the senior management team and a consultant to the organization on information issues.

Practical examples: Participates in strategic planning in the organization. Participates in bench marking or re-engineering teams. Informs management on copyright issues and monitors compliance with copyright law. Negotiates contracts with database vendors. Obtains patent information. Develops information policies for the organization.

2. Personal Competencies

The special librarian...

2.1 is committed to service excellence.

Practical examples: Seeks out performance feedback and uses it for continuous improvement. Conducts regular user surveys. Asks library users if they found what they were looking for. Celebrates own success and that of others. Takes pride in a job well done. Shares new knowledge with others at conferences and in the professional literature. Uses the research knowledge base of special librarianship as a resource for improving services.

2.2 seeks out challenges and sees new opportunities both inside and outside the library.

Practical examples: Takes on new roles in the organization that require an information leader. Uses library-based knowledge and skills to solve a variety of information problems in a wide range of settings, both for individuals or for organizations. Does not limit the library collection or the information search to traditional media such as books and journals.

2.3 sees the big picture.

Practical examples: Recognizes that information-seeking and use is part of the creative process for individuals and for organizations. Sees the library and its information services as part of the bigger process of making informed decisions. Gives the highest priority to urgent demands that are critical to the organization's competitive advantage. Monitors major business trends and world events. Anticipates trends and pro-actively realigns library and information services to take advantage of them.

2.4 looks for partnerships and alliances.

Practical examples: Seeks alliances with management information systems (MIS) professionals to optimize complementary knowledge and skills. Provides leadership on the information management team. Forms partnerships with other libraries or information services inside or outside the organization to optimize resource sharing. Seeks alliances with database vendors and other information providers to improve products and services. Seeks alliances with researchers in faculties of library and information studies to conduct research.

2.5   creates an environment of mutual respect and trust.

Practical examples: Treats others with respect and expects to be treated with respect in return. Knows own strengths and the complementary strengths of others. Delivers on time and on target and expects others to do the same. Creates a problem-solving environment in which everyone's contribution is valued and acknowledged.

2.6   has effective communications skills.

Practical examples: Listens first and coaches staff and others to develop their own solutions. Supports and participates in mentorship programs and succession planning. Runs meetings effectively. Presents ideas clearly and enthusiastically. Writes clear and understandable text. Requests feedback on communications skills and uses it to make improvements.

2.7   works well with others in a team.

Practical examples: Learns about the wisdom of teams and seeks out opportunities for team participation. Takes on responsibility in teams both inside and outside the library. Mentors other team members. Asks for mentoring from others when it is needed. Constantly looks for ways to enhance own performance and that of others through formal and informal learning opportunities.

2.8   provides leadership.

Practical examples: Learns about and cultivates the qualities of a good leader and knows when to exercise leadership. Can share leadership with others or allow others to take the leadership role. Exercises leadership within the library and as a member of other teams or units within the organization. Acknowledges the contribution of all members of the team.

2.9   plans, prioritizes and focuses on what is critical.

Practical examples: Recognizes that in order to use resources most effectively, that ongoing, careful planning is required. Develops an approach to planning and time management that incorporates personal and professional goals. Reviews goals on a regular basis, prioritizes them and make sure that an appropriate proportions of daily activities are related to the most critical personal and professional goals. Mentors others to do the same.

2.10   is committed to lifelong learning and personal career planning.

Practical examples: Committed to a career that involves ongoing learning and knowledge development. Takes personal responsibility for long-term career planning and seeks opportunities for learning and enrichment. Advocates for an approach that encourages and supports ongoing knowledge development and that values the contribution of people. Maintains a strong sense of self-worth based on the achievement of a balanced set of evolving personal and professional goals.

2.11   has developed personal business skills and creates new opportunities.

Practical examples: Recognizes that, in the changing world or work, entrepreneurship and the ability to function as a small business professional are essential skills. Seeks out opportunities to develop these skills. Willing to take employment in a variety of forms including full-time, contract and project work. Uses the entrepreneurial spirit in the organizational environment to revitalize products and services.

2.12   recognizes the value of professional networking and solidarity.

Practical examples: Active in SLA and other professional associations. Uses these opportunities to share knowledge and skills, to bench mark against other information service providers and to form partnerships and alliances. Recognizes the need for a forum where information professionals can communicate with each other and speak with one voice on important information policy issues, such as copyright and the global information infrastructure.

2.13   is flexible and positive in a time of continuing change

Practical examples: Willing to take on different responsibilities at different points in time and to respond to changing needs. Maintains a positive attitude and helps others to do the same. Never says it cannot be done. Looks for solutions. Helps others to develop their new ideas by providing appropriate information. Always on the lookout for new ideas. Sees and uses technology as an enabler of new information ideas, products and services.

Conclusion

These are the competencies of special librarians for the 21st century. They have their roots in the past, but they reach far into the future. Special librarians recognize the expanding nature of the challenges that face them in the information age and the range of competencies that are required to meet them. The challenges represented by these competencies must be seized and acted upon today in order to ensure that special librarians have a viable tomorrow.

The Special Committee on Competencies hopes that this document will evolve and grow through continuing discussion of our expanding base of knowledge and skills.

We encourage SLA members to share additional practical examples of what they do with their competencies so that we can continue to learn from each other and celebrate our achievements. An Executive Summary of this document is available on the SLA website (www.sla.org) and a printed paper brochure from SLA headquarters (1-202-234-4700).

References and Bibliography

Note: This list contains items that are cited in the document as well as background reading on the competencies of special librarians, the value of special libraries and the changing nature of the field.

American Library Association. Guidelines for the Accreditation of Master's programs in Library and Information Studies. Chicago: ALA, 1992.

Association for Library Collections and Technical Services (ALCTS) Educational Policy Statement. Chicago: ALA, 1995.

Bender, David R "Choosing Our Future." Journal of Educational Media and Library Sciences 30(4), summer 1993, 325-31.

Casey, Vicki. "Profession for the Millennium." Information Highways, December 1995, 17.

CRISTAL-ED Mailing List. School of Library and Information Studies, University of Michigan.
Majordomo@sils.umich.edu
http://http2.sils.umich.edu/Publications/CRISTALED/listserv.html

Culnan, Mary J. "What Corporate Librarians Will Need to Know in the Future." Special Libraries 77(4), Fall 1986, 213-16.

Dickerson, Mary E., Chair, et al. Presidential Study Commission on Professional Recruitment, Ethics and Professional Standards. The PREPS Commission Report. Washington, DC: SLA, 1992.

Drabenstott, Katherine M. "Analytical Review of the Library of the Future." College and Research Libraries, 56(1), January 1995, 89-90.

Drake, Miriam A. "A Special Library Perspective". Association of Research Libraries: Proceedings of the 124th Annual Meeting, 1994, p.33-36.

Fisher, William and Matarazzo James. "Professional Development for Special Librarians: Formal Education and Continuous Education for Excellence." In Hill, Linda L., Issue Editor. Education for Library and Information Management Careers in Corporate Environments. Library Trends, 42(2), Fall

1993, 290-303.

Griffiths, Jose-Marie and King, Donald W. Special Libraries: Increasing the Information Edge. Washington, D.C.: SLA, 1993.

Harris, Gwen and Marshall, Joanne G. "Building a Business Case for Special Library Services: The Case of Current Awareness." Special Libraries. 87(3), Summer 1996, 181-94.

Hill, Linda L., Issue Editor. "Education for Library and Information Management Careers in Corporate Environments." Library Trends, 42(2), Fall 1993, 225-365.

Horton, Forrest Woody Jr. Extending the Librarian's Domain: A Survey of Emerging Occupation Opportunities for Librarians and Information Professionals. Washington, DC: SLA, 1994. (SLA Occasional Paper Series Number Four)

Hunt, Patrick J. "Interpreters as Well as Gatherers: The Librarian of Tomorrow ... Today." Special Libraries 86(3), Summer 1995, 195-204.

Johnston, William B. and Arnold H. Packer. Workforce 2000: Work and Workers for the 21 st Century. Indianapolis: Hudson Institute, 1987.

Keating, Michael. "Corporate Virtual Library: Model for the 1990s." Business and Finance Division Bulletin, SLA, 97, Fall 1994, 27.

Kellogg Coalition on Reinventing Information Science, Technology and Library Education (CRISTAL-ED) Project. School of Library and information Studies, University of Michigan.
http://http2.sils.umich.edu/Publications/CRISTALED/KelloggHomePage.html

Keyes, Alison M. "The Value of the Special Library: Review and Analysis." Special Libraries 86(3), Summer 1995, 172-87.

Koenig, Michael E.D. "Educational Requirements for a Library Oriented Career in Information Management." Library Trends 42(2), Fall 1993, 277-89.

Malinconico, S. Michael. "What Librarians Need to Know to Survive in an Age of Technology". Journal of Education for Library and Information Science 33, Summer, 1992. 226-40.

Martin, Susan K. "Achieving the Vision: Rethinking Librarianship." Journal of Library Administration 19(3/4): 209-27, 1993.

Marshall, Joanne G. The Impact of the Special Library on Corporate
Decision-Making. Washington, DC: SLA, 1993.

Massey-Burzio, Virginia "Education and Experience: Or, the MLS is Not
Enough." RSR: Reference Services Review. 19(1), 1991, 72-72.

Medical Library Association. Platform for Change: The Educational Policy
Statement of the Medical Library Association. Chicago: MLA, 1992.

Medical Library Association. Using Scientific Evidence to Improve
Information Practice: The Research Policy Statement of the Medical Library
Association. Chicago: MLA, 1995.

Moulton, Lynda W. "Results of Survey on Professional Development/Graduate
Education for Information Professionals." Library Management Division
Quarterly, SLA, 17(4), Fall 1994, 11-13.

Moulton, Lynda W. "Under Assault? ... Offense, the Best Strategy." Library
Management Division Quarterly, SLA, 18(1), Spring 1995, 14.

Mount, Ellis, ed. Opening New Doors: Alternative Careers for Librarians.
Washington, DC: SLA, 1993.

Murphy, Marcy. The Managerial Competencies of Twelve Corporate Librarians.
Washington, DC: SLA, 1988. (SLA Research Series, Number Two)

Murphy, Marcy. "Preface." In Special Libraries Association. Future
Competencies of the Information Professional. Washington, DC: SLA, 1991.
(SLA Occasional Paper Series, Number One), v-vi.

National Library of Medicine (U.S.). Planning Panel on the Education and
Training of Health Sciences Librarians. The Education and Training of
Health Sciences Librarians. Bethesda, MD: National Institutes of Health,
National Library of Medicine, 1995.

Ojala, Marydee. "Core Competencies of Special Librarians of the Future."
Special Libraries, 84(4), Fall 1993, 230-34.

Ojala, Marydee. "What Will They Call Us in the Future?" Special Libraries
84(4), Fall 1994, 226-29.

Paris, Marion and White, Herbert S. "Mixed Signals and Painful Choices:
The Education of Special Librarians". Special Libraries 77(4), Fall 1986,
207-12.

Piggott, Sylvia E.A. "Why Corporate Librarians Must Reengineer the Library for the New Information Age". Special Libraries 86(1), Winter 1995, 11.

Powell, Ronald R and Raber, Douglas. "Education for Reference/Information Service: A Qualitiatative and Quantitative Analysis of Basic Reference Courses." The Reference Librarian 43, 1994, 145-72.

Ray, Ron. "Crucial Critics of the Information Age." Library Journal 118(7): April 1, 1993, 46-49.

Remeikis, Lois A. "Knowledge Management -- Roles for Information Professionals." Business and Finance Division Bulletin, SLA, 101, Winter 1996,41-43.

Seiss, Judith. "If I Ruled the World, Library Schools Would..." Searcher 2(7), September 1994, 14-16.

Special Libraries Association. Future Competencies of the Information Professional. Washington, DC: SLA, 1991. (SLA Occasional Paper Series, Number One)

Special Libraries Association. Graduate Education Position Statement. Washington, DC: Professional Development Committee, SLA: 1992. (Reviewed every two years and updated if necessary)

Special Libraries Association. SLA Research Agenda. Washington, DC: SLA, 1989.

Special Libraries Association. "Objectives for Special Libraries." Special Libraries, 55(10), December 1964, 671-80. (Reprinted as a brochure by SLA)

Special Libraries Association. Vision Statement. Washington, DC: SLA, 1989.

Special Libraries Association. A Visionary Framework for the Future: SLA's Strategic Plan, 1990-2005. Washington, DC: SLA, 1989.

Spiegelman, Barbara M. "If Practitioners Ruled the World: Suggested Topics for SLA Research." Presented at the conference, The Future of Research for the Special Library Community, March, 1995, Chicago, IL.

Tilson, Y. "Income Generation and Pricing in Libraries." Library Management 51 (2), 1994, 517.

White, M.D. and Abels, E.G. "Measuring Service Quality in Special Libraries: Lessons from Service Marketing". Special Libraries 86(1), Winter 1995, 36-45.

Williamson, Joan. "One-person Libraries and Information Units: Their Education and Training Needs". Library Management 9(5), 1-72, 1988.

Zink, Steven D. "Will Librarians Have a Place in the Information Society?" RSR: Reference Services Review 19(1), 1991, 76-77.

Making Room *for the* Virtual Office

*Providing flexible work options for employees
can boost productivity while still keeping
member service your top priority.*

By Tobi A. Brimsek, CAE, and David R. Bender, Ph.D.

The workforce is changing, and with it, the workplace. As new technologies make it possible for employees to work from a variety of venues, the definition of an office and its appearance are undergoing reconstruction. Then too, the off-site workforce is becoming an increasingly practical player in an evolving work world when you consider that many associations are expanding their presence on a global scale, perhaps requiring satellite work locations. And flexible work options can allow for greater productivity from employees with disabilities or recuperating from temporary injuries or illness by decreasing days missed at the office.

At the Special Libraries Association, Washington, D.C., various factors contributed to SLA's willingness to provide new work options for its employees:
• increasingly varied staff travel and work schedules;
• management understanding of the general direction of the modern workforce and the need to put technology to work to enhance productivity;
• implementation of state-of-the-art workplace technology at SLA; and
• interest in allowing staff members flexibility in terms of work sites.

To that end, SLA developed guidelines for working off-site by first determining how to successfully apply such options *at SLA.* (See sidebar, "Guidelines for Telecommuting and Working at Virtual Offices.") SLA is an international professional association with a staff of 39 serving a growing

HIGHLIGHTS

• PARAMOUNT TO THE success of any new work option is the seamless blend of physical location and member service.
• WORKING OFF-SITE is not an option that fits all work situations—or all workers.
• RAISING SECURITY concerns ensures that staff members are reminded of appropriate computing practices.
• THOUGHT MUST be given to the liability of maintaining equipment off-site or the risk of transporting equipment.

membership of more than 15,000. As with most associations, paramount to the success of any new work option is the seamless blend of physical location and member service.

Perhaps most popular among today's flexible work options is telecommuting, which itself includes the possibility of working from home or from other remote locations by using computers and modems and e-mail, voice mail, and facsimile capabilities to maintain an electronic connection to the association and to its members. However, because working off-site can include undertaking assignments other than those requiring an electronic connection, for the pur-

Guidelines for Telecommuting and Working at Virtual Offices

Definitions

Telecommuting: Staff working from off-site locations from time to time and communicating with office via phone, fax, or modem.

Working off-site: Working off-site on occasion to deal with special circumstances.

At the Special Libraries Association, telecommuting and working off-site are considered to be occasional operation modes requiring the prior approval of the appropriate EDAT supervisor. *[See main text for an explanation of SLA's Executive Director's Advisory Team.]*

Background

SLA's goal is to make technology work for the association and to create working conditions that will increase productivity and reflect the developing working environment in the 1990s while continuing to provide quality service to our membership. Working off-site requires a significant amount of self-discipline. In addition, staff working off-site must be reachable, and their work product must be discernible. The fundamental philosophy behind this concept is that it is a privilege, not a right. The following guidelines are intended to ensure a consistent level of application.

Conditions

1. Duration and approval.

A. Telecommuting or working off-site is on an occasional basis, as approved by the appropriate EDAT supervisor.

B. While the arrangement most often will be prearranged, a request may be approved on short notice to meet a specific need.

2. Authority and responsibilities.

A. There will be an agreement between the staff member and EDAT supervisor regarding the specific tasks that will be accomplished.

B. Working outside the office does not preclude staff responsibility for responding to phone messages or e-mail messages, where applicable.

C. A virtual office does not carry with it virtual hours. Specifically, staff members will be available for consultation during their established work hours, unless otherwise agreed upon in advance.

3. Equipment.

A. Equipment issued for telecommuting purposes will remain the property of the Special Libraries Association. It may not be used by other individuals. The staff member will execute an acknowledgement of receipt of equipment, as appropriate.

B. SLA equipment will not be used for individual needs without prior consent.

4. Security.

A. Security procedures for telecommuting must be adhered to in the strictest sense.

1. No passwords will be divulged or shared.

2. File transfer privileges will be granted on an as-needed basis.

3. Antiviral software will be installed and used each time external data are brought into the PC that connects to SLA.

4. No network access will be permitted during nightly backups, unless a critical need is approved.

5. Under no circumstances shall data be brought into the network from external sources without the knowledge of, consent of, and procedures to be executed by the manager of computer services.

6. No software will be loaded into the network from external sources.

B. As appropriate, staff members will advise their supervisors of any SLA property and/or documents being removed from the headquarters building.

5. Review.

Telecommuting or working off-site will be reviewed on an ongoing basis by the appropriate EDAT supervisor to assess the impact on the position and the association.

6. Revocation of privileges.

Telecommuting or working off-site privileges will be revoked without recourse if the guidelines and requirements outlined in this document are breached in any way. At that time, all SLA property is to be returned immediately to the headquarters office.

pose of this article, *working off-site* will be used to include, but not be limited to, telecommuting options.

Who can do what, where

Working off-site doesn't fit all work situations—or all workers. One of the

The Results of a "Telework" Study

A study conducted earlier this year on the "human dimension" of telecommuting cites a number of factors driving the growth of telecommuting:

• economic trends toward downsizing forcing companies to look for ways to cuts costs, which may translate into reduced office space and on-site resources;

• increasing market competition requiring immediate access to information and constant availability to customers, in turn requiring extended work days—demands that may be easier to accommodate outside the traditional office setting;

• faster and better technology allowing employees to work from remote locations more cost-effectively and with greater ease; and

• greater emphasis being placed on hiring and retaining qualified workers, which often means dipping into a labor pool that requires greater flexibility, such as working parents and people with limited mobility.

The study, conducted for Bell Atlantic by Lamar Reinsch, professor of management communications for the Georgetown School of Business, Georgetown University, Washington, D.C., took place between March and June of this year. Those polled were 103 telecommuters and 20 managers. The study included interviews with 70 of those participants exploring issues of trust, productivity, corporate loyalty, and management's ability to supervise workers to clarify the effects of telecommuting

on manager-worker relationships. Participating Bell Atlantic customers included Fannie Mae, American Express, Bellcore, and Marriott International.

Three quarters of the participating telecommuters said they were "more productive" when telecommuting; one third said they experienced "no disadvantages" in telecommuting. Among the disadvantages most frequently cited were 1) fear of being left out of communication; 2) difficulty in reaching management when there was a problem; and 3) incompatible technologies.

Not surprisingly, the study's recommendations for managing the telecommuting process included not overlooking the importance of communication and training of employees, providing adequate technological support, and moving away from a traditional hierarchical management structure to a more fluid and interdependent paradigm. According to the study, those best equipped to deal with telecommuting are those who can cooperate across hierarchical levels. Likewise, good telecommuters must be able to think independently and direct themselves.

Bottom line, says the study, telecommuting should continue to result in productivity gains for employers and lifestyle gains for workers, who are allowed more time with families, are likely to experience less stress associated with commuting, and may realize greater choice in the future in terms of where they work and live.

first issues to consider is the working style of the staff member. Working outside the office may not be best suited for someone who isn't self-directed.

Likewise, not all activities lend themselves to an off-site work arrangement. Projects entailing heavy writing or phone-calling, for instance, lend themselves well to alternate work sites, while a role that requires meetings half the day with other staff members, suppliers, or association leaders does not.

At SLA, all off-site work arrangements are approved by a member of the SLA Executive Director's Advisory Team. EDAT consists of SLA's executive director, the associate executive director, the assistant executive director of information services, and the assistant executive director of finance and administration. All SLA staff positions are at some level reportable to at least one of these four positions.

EDAT serves in an oversight capacity for guideline implementation. Each off-site work assignment is reviewed on a case-by-case basis, and an agreement, usually verbal, is established between the employee and the appropriate EDAT supervisor regarding work product and expectations. Ongoing review of alternative work options is built into the process to determine the impact of such arrangements on SLA operations.

Technology, security, and cost considerations

Technology. Germane to SLA's ability to begin allowing staff to telecommute was the issue of technological capability. In 1992, SLA underwent a computer conversion from a mainframe system to a local area network. SLA initially opted to have staff use their own computers, modems, and so forth. However, after developing the guidelines and determining the association's ability to recycle equipment through its computer equipment replacement plan, limited loaner equipment is now available. (In addition to guidelines for working off-site, SLA has network guidelines that set forth the rules and regulations governing the use of the SLA computer system and hardware.)

Security. Raising security concerns within the guidelines ensures that staff members are reminded of appropriate computing practices and that telecommuting schedules need to blend with association operations. For example, staff are expected not to dial into the network during certain evening hours because of network backup schedules and maintenance operations.

Cost. Providing flexible work options doesn't come without cost. Financial implications for equipment and utilities, such as phone lines, must be considered. Key questions include these: How many staff are you able to allow to dial into your system simultaneously? When staff members are traveling, do you want them to connect to the office? For instance, upgrading a hotel room to one with a data line or with international telephone connections usually entails a premium.

Standard operating issues enter the cost arena as well. Thought must be given to the liability of maintaining equipment off-site or the risk of transporting it. Issues that aren't so obvious must also be discussed. For example, from an insurance perspective, what must be done about potential employee injuries at off-site locations?

The SLA virtual office

The future for alternative work options at SLA looks bright. To date, approximately 20 percent of SLA's staff has experienced some form of off-site work arrangement—from the executive office to government relations to computer services to finance and administration to professional development to information

Working off-site

(Continued from page 74)

services—at a variety of staff levels. As we provide an even stronger technological backbone, it is inevitable that we will pursue alternative work options to maximize their effectiveness within the organization. With established guidelines for working off-site, the mechanism is in place to provide procedures around which employee–employer work agreements can strike a balance between staff needs and employment obligations in a way that is beneficial to the staff, the organization, and its members.

Tobi A. Brimsek, CAE, is assistant executive director of information services for the Special Libraries Association, Washington, D.C. She is a member of the ASAE Communication, International, and Technology Sections. David R. Bender is SLA's executive director. He holds a doctorate in curriculum, foundations, and higher education administration.

Telecommuting

Defintion: The term "telecommuting" refers to work arrangements in which tasks that are customarily done in an office are done at the employees' homes or at some other off-site location. The most common telecommuting situation involves workers who are linked to the office by telephone, fax machine, and personal computer.

Telecommuters can be full- or part-time employees, and the arrangements can be either temporary or permanent.

Most telecommuters are mid- to upper-mid-level professionals, administrators, technical employees, and clerical workers. Positions that seem well-suited to telecommuting include typing, data entry, writing, editing, and telemarketing. Such jobs involve a great deal of independent work and frequently require little face-to-face contact with other people.

Telecommuting offers workers a flexible situation that can accommodate a variety of working styles. Employees with such arrangements sometimes are free to work the hours that they choose as long as they establish core hours during which the employer and co-workers can contact them.

It is estimated that between 250 and 350 firms nationwide offer this work-time option.

Variations/Features: Variations of telecommuting arrangements include the following:

* Satellite work centers: Employees work from a remote extension of the employer's office.

* Neighborhood work centers: Employees work from a satellite office shared by several different employers.

* Nomadic executive offices: Executives who travel extensively maintain control over projects through use of telephone, fax, and modem-linked computers.

Benefits: Working at home can give employees more flexibility in scheduling personal activities, improve morale and job satisfaction, and provide greater employment opportunities for the handicapped. For employers, telework's benefits include:

* Improved recruitment efforts -- This alternative work arrangement

can help employers expand their labor pool by making it easier for them to hire persons with disabilities and persons who care for children or early retirees. Being able to recruit workers who otherwise might not be available is essential where qualified workers are in short supply.

* Cost containment -- Telecommuting options reduce the need for office space in expensive downtown areas.

* Employees who do not wish to relocate when a company moves to another city or state can nonetheless continue to work for the firm long-distance.

* Increased productivity -- Employees who telecommute work when their energy levels are highest, they are at their most productive, and they are not distracted by co-workers or office politics.

* Sick leave may be decreased because employees who are slightly ill and who would not be able to travel to work would nonetheless feel well enough to work at home. In other situations, employees who have sick dependents at home would still be able to work.

Special Considerations: Telecommuting can increase organizational flexibility and responsiveness and provide a solution to certain employee problems (e.g., commuting), but it is not problem-free for the employer or employee.

To help employers compensate for their inability to visually monitor workers, some firms have turned to electronic monitoring (as in checking via computer to see how many hours a worker is logged on to the company PC) or adopted a management-by-objective approach, which rewards workers based on what they produce, not by the time spent at a task.

Workers also voice concerns about isolation from co-workers, loss of opportunities for promotion because they are unaware of openings, and blurring of workday and home life.

To avoid or minimize potential difficulties, employers interested in implementing telecommuting programs should:

* Carefully select the jobs and individuals who participate in the programs. Consider such factors as the level of concentration required by the job and the need for face-to-face interaction.

* Train both telecommuters and their managers to understand their respective roles and job responsibilities. If necessary, prepare a written agreement that is signed by the telecommuter and approved by the employee's boss.

* To provide support, link telecommuters to the central or headquarters office through a "buddy" system.

* Pay attention to technical details. Make sure remote-location workers have all the necessary telecommunications tools, equipment, and supplies they need to do their jobs well.

* Set flexible guidelines for communication with the headquarters office.

* Develop a system for monitoring and evaluating work of non-management employees. For example, consider using computer software programs to monitor output.

* Provide proper compensation for the work performed. In addition, reimburse telecommuters for all work-related expenses.

* Review state and federal wage-hour and tax laws to avoid legal problems. Although there are no federal laws specific to the telecommuter, general guidelines for work-at-home arrangements are set by the [29 USC 201] Fair Labor Standards Act , IRS regulations, and the Labor Department's "homework" regulations. Some states, including California and Florida, have enacted legislation that formalizes telecommuting arrangements.

* Telecommuting can save employees time and energy commuting, creating a more contented, productive workforce, finds a report by the Commerce Department's National Institute of Standards and Technology. The report notes that about 5 million employees cur- rently use an alternate workplace one day a week or more.

The flexible workplace arrangements telecommuting provides have proven they can help employers recruit and retain key personnel, increase accessibility for all workers, improve office productivity, increase the use of new technology, and reduce costs, according to the report. Meanwhile, employees benefit through increased job satisfaction, reduced commuting time and transportation costs, diminished stress, and increased time and energy for their family life, the report adds, noting that there is a strong correlation between employee satisfaction and customer satisfaction.

A number of large employers have shifted large segments of their workforce, particularly in sales and financial management, to telecommuting arrangements in the last few years, the report says. As the number of employees that telecommute increases at organizations, employers can redesign their principal offices for more intermittent use and generate savings to offset telecommuting participation costs, the report concludes. (Promoting Telecommuting: An Application of the National Information Infrastructure. NIST Special Publication No. 868. U.S. Government Printing Office, Washington, D.C. 20402; (202)

* Workplace flexibility, the balance of work and home, and economic influences are the driving forces behind the use of telecommuting, according to a report by The Conference Board. Based on a survey of 155 employers, the report notes that government mandates also will become a major impetus for telecommuting as the Clean Air Act is enacted.

Employers have become increasingly responsive to flexible work arrangements, the report says, with 72 percent of respondents currently providing telecommuting options for their employees. Forty-two percent of respondents offer telecommuting options to all employees, while half offer it to supervisors and managers only. Among employers that offer the practice, 33 percent have a formal telecommuting policy, 54 percent offer ad-hoc arrangements, and 13 percent have pilot programs, the report adds.

Despite the high availability of telecommuting programs, however, employee utilization is low, the report finds. Indeed, the majority of respondents say that only 1 percent of their total work force participates. The likely reasons for low utilization of telecommuting programs is a lack of available data on the many incidences of ad-hoc arrangements, corporate culture or management resistance, employee fear of negative career consequences, and inappropriateness for the job, the report maintains.

Regarding the costs of telecommuting programs, the report reveals that more than two-thirds (68 percent) of respondents cover the full cost -- including computer, phone, supplies, and related expenses -- but coverage depends primarily on the need and the resources available. Initial costs for telecommuting programs are rated as moderate by the majority of respondents, while 20 percent rate them high and 14 percent say they are insignificant. Ongoing costs are much lower, the report adds, with 71 percent of respondents stating they are insignificant and 28 percent claiming they are moderate.

The major benefits telecommuting provides to employers include improved individual productivity (cited by 47 percent of respondents), greater support of diversity initiatives (42 percent), increased retention of valuable employees (40 percent), and increased employee loyalty (36 percent), the report says. The greatest challenges, meanwhile, include management resistance and skepticism (75 percent of respondents), control (67 percent), equity (45 percent), and culture change (41 percent), the report notes.

Overall, the report concludes, the experience of employers that offer telecommuting programs provides the following advice on promoting successful telecommuting arrangements:

* Telecommuting arrangements require that the needs of all involved are met, especially those of the customers;

Telecommuting: Company Examples

EXAMPLE: American Telephone & Telegraph Co. instituted a telecommuting policy in late 1992, following successful trial efforts in 1989 in Arizona and California. The company had begun experimenting with telecommuting initially to "restore a balance between work- place and family obligations," a representative explains, adding, however, that environmental issues and a concern to reduce vehicle-related air pollution and traffic congestion have also impelled the company to try telecommuting. Currently, more than 22,000 AT & T employees are experienced telecommuters; many have formal agreements covering their short-term or ongoing work-at-home arrangements. The effects of these arrangements have been very positive, the company maintains, citing increased productivity, improved employee morale, increased loyalty, and reports of reduced stress as workers have achieved a better balance between their work lives and family demands.

On September 20, 1994, AT & T sponsored a "telecommuting day" in which approximately 13 percent of the workforce, from 46 states and the District of Columbia, participated. Some 7,500 managers worked from "virtual offices," traveling with six-pound briefcases stocked with cellular phones, notebook computers, and modems connected to customized communications networks.

As part of this first national work-at-home day, AT & T telecommuters participated in a call-in survey to measure the environmental effects of and employees' opinions on telecommuting.

EXAMPLE: Pacific Bell, a San Francisco employer of more than 68,000 workers, began a telecommuting program in April 1985 for a small group of managers. By July 1986, some 90 programmers, analysts, engineers, marketing planners, project managers, external affairs managers, and forecas ters were working at remote sites or at their homes throughout California. Today, among the company's 16,000 salaried employees, 1,500 telecommute.

Managers in every department are encouraged to work at home or at "satellite" offices (small, geographically dispersed locations with limited support facilities), according to PacBell's director of telecommuting programs. Those who wish to participate in the formal, voluntary program are given an overview of telecomm uting and asked to complete a questionnaire. Subsequently, they attend a half-day telecommuting orientation class that covers such issues as scheduling, physical work arrangements, possible business problems, job responsibilities, and potential hazards and benefits of telecommuting. A written work agreement then is prepared by the legal department and signed. Next, the telecommuters are equipped with a variety of personal computers, telephone modems, and communications software packages that let them send and receive information to and from the workplace. The remote workers, who receive the same compensation and benefits as in-office employees, have access to a centralized administrative support group and are paired with a "buddy" at headquarters who can help them with job-related questions. All work-related expenses are paid by the company.

Telecommuting, stresses the telecommuting director, is an "economical, practical, and ex tremely flexible" work-time option that's good for employees and good for the company. Workers have greater flexibility over their work hours and workplace, which translates into reduced commuting time and costs, reduced job stress, increased job opportunities, and improved family relationships. For the employer, telecommuting means increased productivity, decreased absenteeism and turnover, reduced overhead costs, improved recruitment and retention, and new or expanded labor pools.

Pacific Bell is a sponsor of the Telecommuting WorkCenter, Riverside County, Calif., which opened in November 1991. The largest such center in California, the WorkCenter can accommodate as many as 55 employees a day, offering them an alternative to their customary three-hour round-trip commutes to jobs in Orange and Los Angeles counties. Comprising more than 8.800 square feet, the WorkCenter contains both private and secure offices, cubicles, conference rooms, telephone and voice mail services, secure data transmission service, access to personal computers, modems, and printers, photocopying and fax services, a lunch room, exercise facilities, free parking, and office management.

The center is the result of legislation, enacted on behalf of the Riverside County Transportation Commission, that provides state funds for a public-private partnership to operate a telecommuting work center, the goa l of which is to demonstrate the advantages of "moving work to people, not people to work." The Riverside County Economic Development Partnership manages the center; operating expenses are underwritten by the public-private partnership. In addition to Pacific Bell, sponsors include Southern California Edison; organizations that have contributed equipment or professional services include IBM, Stockwell & Binney, Xerox, Thomas, Luebs & Mort, South Coast Air Quality Management Distri ct, and the City of Riverside.

A minimal fee, including telephone service and some work supplies, is paid by participating employers. Currently, TRW, Pacific Bell, Southern California Edison, and IBM, all of which have offices in Orange and Los Angeles counties, permit employees to telecommute from the WorkCenter. Telecommuters may report to the center from one to five days a week, depending on their employer's needs. (Connections, December 1991, 140 New Montgo mery St., San Francisco, Calif. 94105)

EXAMPLE: At least 100 knowledge workers at Travelers Insurance participate in a formal telecommuting program, positions for which are advertised through the company's internal job posting system. Some of the teleworkers are regular part-timers.

Both homeworkers and their managers receive orientation and training, a telecommuter's handbook or management guide, a workstation catalogue, and technical support for equipment problems. At-home workstations can be set up for wordprocessing or equipped with external data bases and electronic or voice mail components. To ensure good communication between telecommuters and the office, access is provided through the firm's own system and through a public packet network. Work space at home is covered under Travelers' liability insurance policy.

The program, which was instituted after a period of experimentation, offers benefits to the company and employees. Productivity is up, according to one company representative, and certain administrative costs are down because there is less need for work space at the central office. In addition, the labor pool has expanded because the program makes it possible to hire employees who live beyond commuting range. For the telecommuters, the program offers flexible schedules and savings on transportation, clothing, and meals.

EXAMPLE: Optional telecommuting is available to more than 16,000 managers employed by Bell Atlantic's telephone companies and the Philadelphia-based Network Services, Inc. Program participants are provided a second telephone line in their homes, in addition to other equipment, including voice mail, call waiting, call forwarding, message services, and fax machines.

The telecommuting program was instituted following several pilot projects that involved more than 100 managerial employees and lasted more than 18 months. According to a company representative, the pilots produced "dramatic increases in employee productivity" and "improvements in morale, job satisfaction, and quality of personal and family life." In addition, they showed Bell Atlantic how its telephone and other services could be used in the "telecommuting environment" of other companies. What Bell Atlantic discovered, according to the company's representative, was that "many of [its] products and services could stimulate the office environment and help telecommuters make their absence from their offices transparent to clients."

Telecommuting: Survey Data

Hay/Huggins Data on Flexible Work Conditions

A work-at-home or telecommuting policy for exempt employees is in effect at 11 percent of 746 organizations responding to a 1994

Hay/Huggins survey of HR practices at medium- and large-size companies. Implementation of such a policy is being considered by another 3 percent of employers. From 1990 through 1992, the comparable prevalence figure was 14 percent; the figure for the 1994 survey is unchanged since 1993.

Typically, the survey points out, employers offer a work-at-home arrangement "as needed" or establish a telecommuting program to respond to individual employees' requests or to accommodate workers' child care needs. Frequently, employers view flexible work arrangements as a family-oriented benefit that has the added advantage of helping to improve motivation and increase productivity.

Job sharing programs are in place at 11 percent of 449 responding companies. Such programs are most prevalent among financial institutions (19 percent, down from 21 percent in 1993); less so among services firms (11 percent, down from 13 percent in 1993) or industrial organizations (8 percent, up from 7 percent in 1993). The majority of such programs, 57 percent, have been in place only since 1990. Respondents say they institute job sharing programs primarily to attract and retain quality employees and to respond to workers' flexible scheduling requests.

The survey also finds that:

* Employees are allowed to work flexible hours at 42 percent of 702 responding firms. In 92 percent of these companies, all employees are permitted to adopt a flextime schedule. By industry, financial organizations (33 percent of 133 respondents in the industry group) are more likely than either services companies (21 percent of 214 respondents) or industrial firms (15 percent of 355 respondents) to have a flexible hours system in place in all departments.

* Four-day work weeks are scheduled by 28 percent of surveyed organizations. Of these, 75 percent require employees to work the same number of hours as would be worked on a normal five-day schedule.

* Regionally, job sharing programs are more apt to be implemented by employers in the Plains states (21 percent), Central states (19 percent), and Mid-Atlantic region (14 percent) than by companies in the Mountain states and West (9 percent), South (6 percent) or New England (5 percent). Work-at-home or telecommuting policies are more likely to be implemented by organizations in the Mountain states and West (24 percent), the Plains states (17 percent), or the Mid-Atlantic region (16 percent) than by firms in New England (13 percent) or the South (6 percent).

* Generally, the larger the company, the more likely it will have a work-at-home policy. Twenty-four percent of respondents with 10,001 or more employees, but just 13 percent of organizations with fewer than

500 employees, have a work-at-home policy. Telecommuting policies are least prevalent among firms with 1,001 workers to 5,000 workers (12 percent). Job sharing programs are considerably more prevalent in firms with 5,001 workers to 10,000 workers (29 percent) or more than 10,001 employees (31 percent) than in companies with 501 workers to 1,000 employees (6 percent) or fewer than 500 employees (5 percent).

* In 49 percent of 466 responding organizations, exempt employees work different shifts. Fifty-three percent of such workers receive extra compensation for shift work. Of 365 respondents, 51 percent say they schedule overtime for exempt employees. (1994 Hay/Huggins Benefits Report (Vol. I, Prevalence of Benefits Practices and Executive Summary), The Hay Group. 229 S. Rittenhouse Sq., Philadelphia, Pa. 19103; telephone (215) 875-2784 or fax to HHBR Survey Unit at (215) 875-2833; $950)

Olsten Corp. Telecommuting Survey

Telecommuting has become increasingly popular as automation has advanced and employers have acquired the hardware required to enable employees to work, via modem and computer, from remote sites, reports the Olsten Corporation, which offers staffing and training assistance services to business, industry, and government and annually surveys corporate executives on information management trends. In a poll of 423 vice presidents, management information systems executives, and directors of North American businesses participating in the 1995 Olsten Forum Note: for Information Management. Olsten Corporation finds that 49 percent of employers offer or are considering employee telecommuting arrangements, up from 42 percent in 1994 and 39 percent in 1993. One-third (up from 29 percent in 1994 and 27 percent in 1993) report that telecommuting already is in practice.

The greatest users of telecommuting arrangements are insurance companies (54 percent, up from 32 percent in 1994) and high-tech organizations (46 percent, up from 44 percent in 1994). These are followed by services (40 percent, up from 37 percent in 1994). Health care (26 percent), manufacturing (also 26 percent), public and nonprofit agencies (27 percent), and the retail and wholesale sector (30 percent) are least likely to offer or practice telecommuting.

Conducted for the Olsten Corporation by McKendrick & Associates, an independent research firm, the survey also finds that:

* Seven of 10 respondents that report telecommuting activity enable their professional and technical employees to telecommute; approximately one-third also have telecommuting "hookups" for their sales and marketing personnel.

* Telecommuting is most prevalent among companies with multi-platform client/server networks (systems using a central mainframe or mid-range

computers linked to personal computers and local area networks).
Forty-three percent of companies with such networks have a
telecommuting program in place. In contrast, 30 percent of firms that
rely on decentralized local area networks (all processing is on PCs
connected by networks) and 22 percent of organizations with
proprietary centralized systems (all processing is on multi-user
mainframe or mid-range computers that cannot be accessed by PCs) have
telecommuting programs. (Managing Today's Automated Workplace,
Olsten Corp., 175 Broad Hollow Rd., Mail Stop T60, Melville, N.Y.
11747; (516) 844-7800/Media Contact: Middleberg & Associates, 130
East 59th St., New York, N.Y. 10022; (212) 888-6610)

Conference Board Survey on Telecommuting Practices

Employers are increasingly responsive to flexible work arrangements,
including telecommuting arrangements, according to a Conference Board
survey of 155 companies that are representative of the Board's
Work-Family Research and Advisory Panel and that have experience
implementing work-family programs. (NOTE: The survey is not intended
as a representative sample of all companies.) Seventy-two percent of
all the respondents offer telecommuting options to their employees; of
these, 33 percent have a formal telecommuting policy, 13 percent are
conducting a pilot program, and 54 percent have ad hoc arrangements.

Of 122 respondents, 41 percent offer telecommuting companywide; 29
percent restrict the option to certain departments; 14 percent only
allow selected divisions to practice telecommuting; and 11 percent
limit telecommuting to employees at headquarters offices. In half the
firms offering telecommuting options, the flexible work arrangement is
available to all supervisors and managers; in 42 percent, to all
employees; in 37 percent, to exempt employees only; in 22 percent, to
nonexempt employees; in 11 percent, to nonunion workers, and in 2
percent, to union employees.

The survey also finds that:

* Telecommuting costs, including expenses for computer, phone,
supplies, and related costs, are picked up by 68 percent of
respondents. Of 122 firms, two-thirds say initial costs for equipment,
installation, administration, etc., are "moderate"; for 20 percent,
"high"; and for 14 percent, "insignificant." Seventy-one percent of
the companies describe ongoing program costs as "insignificant."

* Program implementation typically is the responsibility of the human
resources department (listed by 51 percent of the respondents),
although managers (32 percent) also are often charged with approving
and overseeing implementation.

* In selecting a telecommuter, 85 percent of 122 respondents indicate
that the "most important consideration" is the type of job or

position; 83 percent say it is "ability to work autonomously"; 75 percent look for "dependability [and ability to] meet deadlines"; and 62 percent make performance evaluation outcomes a deciding factor. In implementing telecommuting, respondents cite among their "top 10 items" selecting self-motivated employees, 54 percent; maintaining open communication, 41 percent; developing formal guidelines, 39 percent; providing equipment and technical support, 37 percent; and senior management support, 31 percent.

* Just 15 percent of the respondents permitting telecommuting have measured their program's effectiveness; however, there appears to be solid enthusiasm for such a work arrangement. Ninety-three percent of 122 respondents claim as one of telecommuting's "greatest advantages" increased flexibility for employees, and 80 percent say telecommuting increases workers' motivation and commitment. Forty-seven percent believe that telecommuting's major benefit to employers is improved individual productivity.

* Management resistance and skepticism are cited by 75 percent of respondents as one of telecommuting's "greatest challenges." Difficulty in supervision, listed by 67 percent of the 122 employers, and employees' difficulty in remaining part of the team, cited by 58 percent of the firms, also are considered problems. ("Work-Family Roundtable: Telecommuting." Vol. 4, No. 1, Spring 1994, The Conference Board. Inc., 845 Third Ave., New York, N.Y. 10022; (212) 759-0900; Customer Orders Department, (800) USBOARD)

Gallup/Accountants on Call Survey on Telecommuting

Employees who work at home are at least as productive as those who work in a traditional office setting, according to more than half of 711 respondents to a survey conducted by the Gallup Organization for Accountants On Call, a placement firm. Of the 711 adults, who work either full- or part-time, 44 percent think that employees who work at home are as productive as office workers; 17 percent believe that those who work at home are more productive than office workers. Nearly a third (31 percent) maintain, however, that employees working at home are less productive than their peers at the office.

The survey also finds that:

* Approximately 27 million employee work at least part-time in their homes.

* Fifty percent of women and 39 percent of men think that employees who work at home are as productive as their office-bound colleagues.

* Thirty-eight percent of workers with a high school education, compared with 51 percent of college-educated employees, say that employees who work at home are as productive as those working in

offices.

* Thirty-seven percent of blue-collar workers, compared with 25 percent of white-collar employees, think that employees working at home are less productive than employees in offices. ("Workers Say Those Working at Home Equal Office Workers in Productivity," BNA's Employee Relations Weekly , Vol. 12, January 24, 1994, p. 100/ Profiles of the American Worker, Accountants on Call, Park 80 West, Plaza II, Garden State Parkway at Interstate 80, 9th Fl., Saddle Brook, N.J. 07622; (201) 843-0006)

LINK Resources Telecommuting Survey

In 1991, some 5.5 million company employees worked at home part- or full-time during normal business hours, according to data included in the sixth annual "National Work-at-Home Survey" conducted by LINK Resources Corp., a New York-based technology research and consulting firm. This figure represents a 38 percent average annual increase over the 1990 figure of 4 million. Of the 1991 total, 876,000 telecommuters worked 35 or more hours per week at home, Monday through Friday, with the remainder working at home an average of slightly fewer than 2.5 days per week. (Data are based on telephone interviews with 2,500 randomly selected U.S. households surveyed in the second quarter of the year, of which 5.4 percent reported that one or more persons qualifies as a telecommuter (a total equal to 4.5 percent of the U.S. civilian workforce aged 18 or older). The 5.5 million figure includes both formal and informal telecommuters, but not self-employed homeworkers. The majority of the 5.5 million telecommuters are in small businesses.)

Telecommuting, the data show, is "growing rapidly" among organizations with more than 1,000 employees, companies with fewer than 10 employees, business executives and managers, and engineers and scientists. Forty-three percent of telecommuters are in executive and professional specialty occupations, and nearly one-fourth are in various manual and low-tech jobs. In the public sector, telecommuters number 240,000, up from 160,000 in 1990.

The typical telecommuter is either male (53.3 percent) or female (46.7 percent), aged 35 to 37, and part of a dual-career (married/couple) household (73.3 percent). In 53 percent of telecommuter 241:399 households, children under 18 are present; in 22 percent, there are children under 6. Many telecommuters not only work during normal business hours, but on weekends and evenings.

The survey also finds that:

* Business professionals (13.3 percent, .73 million) and executives and managers (12.6 percent, .69 million) comprise the leading occupational groups of telecommuters, followed by engineers and

scientists (9.6 percent, .53 million) and salesworkers (6.7 percent, .37 million).

* Computers are owned by more than one-third (36.3 percent) of telecommuter households, compared to 15 percent of households where no homeworker is present. Sixty-eight percent of telecommuters use a personal computer at their regular place of work outside the home, and nearly 10 percent separately bring a PC home from an office monthly or more frequently.

* While the telephone remains the "most important single piece of technology" (70.4 percent of surveyed households own telephone answering machines), computer modems are found in 16 percent of telecommuter households and fax machines are owned by 7 percent.

* Spending by telecommuters for PCs, software, peripherals, fax devices, and telephone services totaled $1.6 billion in 1990, up 14 percent from $1.4 billion in 1989. The total does not reflect investments in other office equipment, furniture, or accessories.

Given current growth rates, the telecommuter population will swell to 11.2 million company employees by 1995, according to LINK's forecast. This strong outlook, LINK says, "reflects a continuation of the current trendline in which part-time telecommuting is the biggest contributor to growth, fueled by the convergence of business and social factors with personal information technologies that make workflow and scheduling more flexible." ("U.S. Telecommuting Population Grows to 5.5 Million," Press Release, March 3, 1992, LINK Resources Corp., 79 Fifth Ave., New York, N.Y. 10003; (212) 627-1500)

The U.S. homeworker population, comprising individuals who perform income-producing or job-related work at home part- or full-time, increased to 38.4 million in 1991, up 12 percent from 34.3 million in 1990, LINK reports. During the period studied, homeworkers spent more than $20 billion on home office products and telephone services.

Based on telephone interviews with 2,500 randomly selected U.S. households, LINK's annual homeworker study also finds that:

* Telecommuters represent the fastest growing segment of homeworkers. Time pressures at home and growing concerns about commuting and air pollution are contributing to the growth of this group.

* Moonlighting, or part-time freelancing by company employees, increased from 9.4 million to 10.5 million from 1990 to 1991, primarily in response to the U.S. recession.

* "High tech" corporate after-hours homeworkers total 10.6 million employees. This figure represents a 5 percent increase over the number of company workers who brought work home in 1990.

* The number of truly self-employed persons (the primary source of income is based on home business activity) has grown by 600,000 households -- a 6 percent rise since 1990. Some 11.8 million Americans fit LINK's description of a "self-employed" individual.

* One of five homeworkers in LINK's universe are defined exclusively by their use of home office products (PCs, modems, fax machines, multiple phone lines for business purposes at home), in contrast to conventional home businesses, hobby businesses, and other traditional forms of homework.

* Portable electronics are proliferating in homeworker households. According to LINK data, more than 13 percent of homeworkers who purchased a PC in 1990 bought a lap-top or notebook model. Overall, 19 percent of homeworker households reported owning pocket electronic organizers or reference devices, and 12 percent reported using cellular telephones. ("U.S. Homeworker Population Jumps to 38.4 Million." Press Release. March 3, 1992, LINK Resources Corp., 79 Fifth Ave., New York. N.Y. 10003; (212) 627-1500)

Medium/Large Company Survey

One in five major U.S. firms now uses telecommuting. according to LINK. In a study of remote work involving telecommunications managers at a representative sample of 500 U.S. firms with 101 to 5.000-plus employees, LINK finds that:

* Mobile workers (e.g.. sales or field representatives) are employed by 62 percent of the firms polled. This figure represents a total of 5.47 million mobile workers in 123.000 medium- and large-size companies nationwide. The average number of employees using this workstyle is 71.6 per company.

* More than half the companies (53 percent) have employees who work after hours at home using any combination of personal computers, modems. fax. or dedicated phone services. This group totals 1.44 million workers. or 22.1 employees per company.

* Informal telecommuting -- defined as work performed by employees at home during normal business hours under informal arrangements between the employees and their supervisors -- occurs in 21 percent of the responding firms. This group comprises 470,000 informal telecommuters. or 18.6 employees per company.

* Remote independent contractors who work from home (230.000 contractors, 9.6 workers per company) are employed by 19 percent of the organizations surveyed.

* Formal telecommuting -- defined as work performed by employees at

home during normal business hours using formal arrangements between the company and the employee -- occurs in 14 percent of the firms. This group totals 240,000 formal telecommuters, or 13.9 employees per company.

* Business services are the most likely to use telecommuting. Thirty-five percent of firms in this sector reported using informal telecommuting; 29 percent, formal telecommuting; and 25 percent, home-based independent contractors.

* Combining its large employer data with its small business data, LINK calculates a total of 3.1 million formal U.S. telecommuters. Of this total, 2.83 million are employees of small businesses, while 240,000 are found among larger companies.

Based on focus group interviews with managers of large organizations involved in the statistical survey, LINK finds that:

* Three factors stand out most as driving the use of remote workstyles in large companies: corporate requirements to improve job performance among sales and knowledge workers; the desire to accommodate employees' needs for work-schedule flexibility; and legislative mandates. "Mobile work and home-based work extend the ability of employees to be productive while traveling and when working after normal business hours, often across time zones." LINK explains. "This means that salesworkers can spend more time with customers and executives can work more after hours while still spending time with their families." In addition, the flexibility provided by remote workstyles often translates into extra enthusiasm and productivity from time-pressured employees who are allowed to work at home, LINK says. Remote work technology also enables employers to respond to needs or requirements to reduce daily commuter traffic and air pollution.

* There is a "substantial and growing commitment" to remote work-support products in medium and large firms. The equipment most often used to perform remote work includes: fax machines (99 percent), modems (98 percent), beepers and pagers (63 percent), cellular phones (56 percent), voice mail (36 percent), and remote local area network access (26 percent). For mobile workers, beepers and cellular phones are important tools; for after-hours workers and telecommuters, fax, modems, and voice mail "play a big role." ("Telecommuting in Major Firms." Press Release. March 3, 1992. LINK Resources Corp., 79 Fifth Ave., New York, N.Y. 10003; (212) 627-1500)

REPRINTED FROM   #2849

PERSONNEL JOURNAL

■ Catalyst Study Sets Work-life Standards

Flexibility Comes Out of Flux

No longer are alternative work arrangements the exclusive domain of mothers. Today, companies such as Bank of Montreal and Price Waterhouse are beginning to accommodate all types of workers with assorted needs. A recent study by Catalyst, "Making Work Flexible: Policy to Practice," provides clues to their success.

By Charlene Marmer Solomon

A decade ago, flexible work schedules were about as common as e-mail. In other words, not very. Progressive companies were touted for their broad-minded policies of part-time and flextime work, and some experimented with telecommuting. Driving these management practices was the magnanimous attitude that women with young children needed greater flexibility if they were to stay in the workforce. It was a benevolent philosophy, not necessarily a business-driven one.

How times have changed.

Today with increasing numbers of organizations offering flexible work arrangements of some type, flexibility is as widely anticipated as a computer with a functioning modem and e-mail capabilities. Although most people continue to work in traditional ways during traditional hours, the idea of flexibility is as common as the sound of a dial tone whirring through a computer. The most sweeping change? No longer are flexible hours and a flexible workplace the domain of young mothers. All types of workers want these options. And, a variety of companies are offering them because they make good business sense.

Flexibility enhances productivity. However dramatic the changes may seem when compared with 10 years ago, the changes within the last few years are evolutionary, not revolutionary. More and more companies continue to experiment with different types of options, accommodating a greater variety of employees through these options. More and more are discovering that in specific cases, these arrangements help with productivity, decrease turnover and reduce employee stress. There are several companies who have offered flexible work arrangements for so long they've moved the effort from a programmatic solution to a more fundamental endeavor that has affected corporate policy and culture.

To measure and propagate the success of such forward-looking companies, Catalyst—the New York City-based workplace think tank—unveiled its most recent report in February of this year, "Making Work Flexible: Policy to Practice." The report is based on a study it initiated in the

Fall of 1994 in which the group identified 31 corporations and professional firms nationally recognized as having exemplary flexible workplace policies and whose motivation wasn't altruistic but business-driven. From confidential telephone interviews and several roundtable discussions, the organization developed guidelines to help other companies create and manage flexibility (see "Making Work Flexible: A Summary"). Among these companies are the Bank of Montreal, Price Waterhouse LLP, KPMG Peat Marwick, Deloitte & Touche LLP, NationsBank, Aetna Life & Casualty, Corning, Steelcase Inc. and Pillsbury.

As Marcia Brumit Kropf, vice president of the Research and Advisory Services division for Catalyst points out, until recently, flexibility was viewed as an issue for women phasing back into full-time work after a maternity leave. Now anyone—male or female—may find work needs affected by obligations outside of work: the care of young children, the needs of school-age children, the care of elderly parents, personal development or community work. And American workers of both genders currently face pressure to work long hours and to put in the *face time* at the office. From the employer's side, flexibility aids in retaining and recruiting valuable employees. It responds to demographic changes in the workforce, reduces turnover, services people in different time zones, meets cyclical or seasonal business demands, provides continuity on projects and in client service, allows operation of a round-the-clock business, and helps maintain morale and performance after reengineering or downsizing.

"The bottom line is to try to recognize and accommodate the needs of a diverse population," says Michael V. Littlejohn, managing director at New York City-based Price Waterhouse LLP. "Flexibility now carries with it a much larger connotation than some of the traditional definitions such as flextime or part-time. It's trying to recognize flexible work arrangements that are more far-

Tips for Going Flexible

Managers often are uncomfortable negotiating and supervising alternative work arrangements. Guidelines and examples of effective procedures help educate them about their benefits and help them negotiate terms and supervise effectively. Below are some practical tips.

ROLE OF THE EMPLOYEE
- Think through which option makes sense and whether that option provides the flexibility you need
- Seek counsel from other individuals who are working flexibly
- Consider how the arrangement might impact your work and the work of your colleagues
- Talk to your manager
- Write your proposal
- Iron out the details
- Send a copy to the appropriate people
- Communicate the new arrangement to appropriate co-workers
- Evaluate the arrangement periodically with your manager

ROLE OF THE MANAGER
- Address business needs
- Assess department needs
- Staff creatively
- Consider each proposal on its own merits
- Seek counsel from colleagues, especially those experienced with flexible work options
- Ask for assistance or guidance from human resources
- Be a coach
- Communicate the new arrangement to other staff in the department
- Monitor the arrangement

ROLE OF THE HR MANAGER
- Identify internal issues and needs surrounding flexible work arrangements
- Identify specific training needs
- Resolve employee-manager conflicts
- Serve as an internal resource
- Communicate and advise on organizational guidelines

Source: Catalyst

reaching."

As if to underscore Catalyst's findings, New York City-based Hewitt Associates LLC unveiled a recent report, "Work and Family Benefits Provided by Major U.S. Employers in 1994," which shows that 66% of the 1,035 organiza-

tions surveyed offered flexible scheduling (up 6% from the year before). Of those, 71% offered flextime, 65% offered part-time, 34% offered job sharing, 21% offered compressed work schedules, 14% offered summer hours and 5% provide other options. Flexible arrangements include two types of options: full-time and reduced-time. Full-time options include flextime (workday begins/ends when employee and manager decide), flexible week (fewer but longer days, shorter days in six-day weeks), or flex place (branch offices, telecommuting). Reduced time options include part-time or job sharing.

But creating company policy is one thing; implementing workable practices can be quite another. Consequently, a key component of the Catalyst report is to highlight organizations that put these principles to work.

Provide a variety of flex options. Toronto-based Bank of Montreal brings together Catalyst's four goals: It builds organizational support for flexibility; it supports managers and users of the practice; it internalizes (or incorporates) the practice, and it sustains the momentum.

The Bank of Montreal has long been a proponent of advancing women throughout its ranks. One example of this is the 1991 Task Force on the Advancement of Women, which was a year-long project sponsored by the bank's president and chief operating officer, Tony Comper. The task force undertook the largest survey of the bank's employees ever. Not only did it uncover myths about women and why they weren't progressing through the organization, but it also provided the basis for developing action plans. The entire flexible work arrangement initiative was an outgrowth of its findings.

"It created an understanding that one of the key things we need to do is to formally support employees—men and women—who are balancing their multiple commitments to work and family, education and community," says Diane Ashton, vice president of employee programs and the office of work place equality. "The connection to the business case is apparent when we look at demographics and understand our workforce and become concerned we don't have enough women making their way through to our senior jobs (policy-, program-, and product-development type of jobs). We realized we were neglecting the talents of half the working population."

As a result, the company developed a policy called *Balancing Multiple Commitments* that incorporates flexibility in many ways: through flextime, flexible workweek, part-time on a permanent basis, job sharing and *flex place*. Flex place allows employees to work two or three days a week in another bank branch that's either closer to home or in a more convenient location. The bank provides this flex space by setting up several workstations at different locations, each with phones, PCs, and other necessities that allow people to work outside of their normal workplace. This also is convenient when someone has appointments with clients that aren't conveniently located to their usual place of work.

The policies are working. At least, they're having the desired effect with regard to encouraging women in their upward movement. For example, the number of female executive officers grew significantly: In 1990, the number increased 6%; in 1991, 9%; and in 1995, 19%.

Furthermore, of the 2,125 positions in the Senior Management Group in October 1991, only 13% were women; exactly four years later the figure had risen to 20.4%.

Ashton herself benefited from the policy when she created an arrangement whereby she worked full time but was paid only for 90% of it. It gave her one half-day a week she saved up. "I used that time to be able to spend more time with my children because they get a lot more time off than our standard four weeks of vacation," she says. "It just enabled me to carry on when there was an emergency. When somebody got chickenpox, I didn't feel like I had to scramble for arrangements." This safety valve relieved the burden.

Build organizational support. The bank combines all of the important factors cited in the Catalyst report. One of the most important features of Bank of Montreal's flexibility approach is that the policy's spirit is incorporated into the strategic development plan and the business plan. Executive-level managers—and all other managers—create objectives for hiring, promoting and retaining people and decide how flexibility will fit into those target plans. These create a baseline. Performance appraisals also include attention to flexibility, with each manager remaining accountable for meeting individual goals.

In other words, both employees and managers are responsible for translating these work arrangements into viable options. For example, employees initiate a proposal that explains why the flex arrangement would make their lives easier and present it to local management. The onus of responsibility, though, lies with the manager to be flexible and open-minded. As a protection for both of them, they define a trial period after which time, they sit down and evaluate it.

This shared responsibility—and trial period—allows employees to generate extraordinary creativity because they can try out different options. For example, a compressed workweek of three days may sound liberating. The bank's operating hours allow this type of work option since many of the branches are open six days a week from 8 a.m. to 8 p.m., allowing employees the option of a Monday, Tuesday, Wednesday shift or a Thursday, Friday, Saturday shift. However, although many employees say they would appreciate it, and believe they've discovered the perfect solution, others may find it an exhausting schedule after trying it for a month.

Since the solutions are employee-generated, employees write a letter to their manager and, once approved, they send a copy to the office of Work Place Equality. This not only establishes the Work Place Equality department as a resource center, it also allows the center to track and understand what people are doing. "The spirit of this policy is that it's employee-initiated," says Ashton. "They come up with the proposal, and it's worked out at a local level between the employee and the manager. This has been one of the strengths of the policy."

Support managers and employees. One way in which the Bank of Montreal propagated its views was through a 100-page book, "Flexing Your Options." It describes the philosophy, policies and procedures of the bank's commitment to flexible work, including a detailed checklist for a basic employee-initiated proposal. It also includes items such as commonly asked questions by managers, sample manager replies and phone numbers for obtaining further information.

To set the tone, before introducing the five flexible options (flextime, flexible workweek, permanent part-time, job sharing, flex place), the first paragraph of the document states, "While such arrangements aren't for everyone, there is compelling evidence that increased self-management translates into increased productivity. The bank is committed to flex arrangements because they make good business sense. The corporate policy, *Balancing Multiple Commitments*, outlines the direct relationship between helping employees balance their commitments to work, family, education and community, and improved employee morale, increased productivity and superior customer service."

Internalize the practice; sustain the commitment. The bank also reinforced its philosophy by accepting these flexible arrangements and by assessing employees' experiences. It believes this practice is important so the arrangements can be tracked for their impact and benefit to the organization. This is one reason the office of Work Place Equality requests a copy of the approved work-arrangement proposal.

Clearly, the bank sustains the commitment by including goals and expectations regarding flexibility in its performance reviews. In fact, employees even rate their managers on this dimension. Each manager's scores (by his or her subordinates) are averaged, and the employees give their boss feedback about the scores.

This integral respect for the concept of flexibility permeates the organization. Therefore, programs are used by individuals in many different situations. For instance, the original intent was to help women advance by relieving some of the family burden (child care time pressures), but others are using it as well: single fathers, for example, or one man who works 40 hours in four days to enable him to spend one day a week leading Boy Scout activities. And, these kinds of arrangements are being used throughout the organization, not just with junior people. Flexibility is permeating the culture. "I know we have senior managers who are either working on a part-time arrangement, compressed workweek or flex place. These aren't people who have been sidelined. They're individuals with important jobs, which is key. We've been able to make flexibility part of the culture. It isn't just seen as something for our most junior people," says Ashton.

Make flexibility a bottom-line issue. Accounting firm Price Waterhouse LLP (PW) also is lauded in the Catalyst study as a company that integrates flexibility companywide. Indeed, PW is redefining its organization because of an increasingly diverse workforce. Fundamental to that is embracing flexibility. Littlejohn, who heads the Office of Diversity Programs as well as national recruitment, says the effort is twofold: both philosophical and concrete. "The effort recognizes and accommodates the needs of a diverse population (a broader definition than women and minorities, it in-cludes single parents, people who have issues with elder care, child care, and others who want more balance between their personal and work lives).

"Flexibility in the firm goes beyond the concrete part-time and flex-work arrangements. It also involves a philosophical perspective." According to Littlejohn, "We're trying to change the mindset of the firm.

"Traditionally, of course, the mindset was that you give 110% to the firm, and if that means a 60- or 70-hour week, so be it. I've seen a distinctive shift over the past couple of years, recognizing the fact we can no longer expect that of our people."

As in the case of the Bank of Montreal, demographics are fueling the

---

Making Work Flexible: A Summary

The purpose of the study, "Making Work Flexible: Policy to Practice," is to provide models for change. Catalyst created a framework of four goals, each with four strategies to develop a flexible work environment:

GOAL I: BUILD ORGANIZATIONAL SUPPORT
- Define and explain the link between flexibility and business goals
- Ensure and communicate senior management support
- Articulate the organization's commitment to flexibility
- Identify and support pilot programs

GOAL II: SUPPORT MANAGERS AND USERS
- Provide tools
- Evaluate effectiveness
- Share models and case studies
- If necessary, revise systems

GOAL III: INTERNALIZE THE PRACTICE
- Incorporate flexibility into other organizational initiatives
- Create and support relationships and networks
- Expand and refine human resources department roles
- Assess the perceptions, experiences, and acceptance of alternative arrangements

GOAL IV: SUSTAIN THE COMMITMENT
- Continually communicate internally about the issues
- Look for ways to promote flexibility externally
- Implement accountability measures
- Review and evaluate the work environment and modify activities accordingly

Source: Catalyst

---

changes. "We have to recognize that as the demographics of society change, so do the firms. For us not only to be productive, but also to be competitive, we have to meet head-on the reality that people have different needs."

Although part-time work options may not seem like such a spectacular innova-

---

tion at first glance, they're indeed challenging for intensely client-focused firms for which on-the-spot service and attention are synonymous with revenue. Consequently, for PW to adapt its philosophy toward traditional ways of working, it had to reconsider the entire notion of work styles and how to service customers effectively while being responsive to employees. In fact, there were two forces at play simultaneously. One was the needs of the employees. The other was the changing needs of the clients, who have become quite diverse in their profiles. The firm also believes that its clients want professionals who reflect their population and, thereby, their concerns.

Technology can support managers and users. One of the tools in PW's network is the company's sophisticated technological infrastructure that allows partners and associates to establish virtual offices. With *Lotus Notes* and voicemail, laptop computers become phones, meeting planners and fax machines, allowing employees to support their clients not only in the client's location, but from anywhere. Technology also has diminished the need for individuals to come into Price Waterhouse offices to transfer information. For example, they previously had to be in the office to have access to files, perform research and provide colleagues with information. No more. Now, most of that can be done remotely via technology.

Given these changes, which facilitate responsiveness to both clients and employees, the company is attempting to extend flexibility in formal and informal ways. PW believes flexible work policies are a powerful tool for attracting and retaining people—a competitive necessity. "Big Six professional services firms face a big challenge because people look at them as a mill—a sweat shop where people work 60- and 80- hour weeks for three or four or five years and we throw them away if we don't make them a partner," says Littlejohn. "We had to create the mindset that we're becoming a kinder place to work; that we'll try our best to accommodate employees' needs."

And, fundamental to that, the firm is

changing some of its values and implementing a new career model. Historically, individuals joined the company shortly after college and worked for eight to 10 years. If they made partner, great. If not, they left the company. It was a rigid career path that allowed no leeway for other options. According to Littlejohn, several problems prompted PW to change the situation. Number one, the firm was losing very good people because they hadn't made partner within the allotted time; number two, employees were saying that partnership wasn't for everyone and alternatives to the partner track would be valued; and number three, clients were expressing the need to have professional service providers who were not only good consultants but also had a depth of knowledge in their specialty. Consequently, the idea of success broadened to include deep technical specialists as well as individuals who wanted a career on the macro level (wanted partnership). Expected time frames also were changed dramatically. Now, there are several career tracks based on the achievement of milestones rather than on the length of time to complete those milestones. Compensation is based accordingly.

Enter the notion of part-time and flex-time arrangements. With these essential changes in the structure of the firm, the flex alternatives become viable. No small thing. This is a fundamental shift in the way Price Waterhouse approaches business and thinks about its employees. It relates to changing the culture of PW.

"Because relationships are such a key in a professional services environment, and our clients are paying us a fee, they have certain expectations," says Littlejohn. We can't just say unequivocally we're going to implement something irrespective of our clients' wishes. It requires us to not only sell our employees on this, but we also have to sell our clients. We have to sell our clients on the fact it's good business for them to have someone onsite four days a week versus five days. It's really in the client's best interest to work for a balance so our people are happy and they're happy."

Communication serves managers and employees. One of the most helpful ways PW communicates its policies is through its newsletters and other organization-wide communication vehicles. It uses these methods to show how flexibility *can* work and achieve business results as well as satisfy individual needs. Via its communication channels, it relates information such as the fact more than 400 people are working flexibly, including 90 managers and two partners. It also encourages the use of these flexible work possibilities by stating the names of people employees can speak with if they're interested in discussing flexibility.

Price Waterhouse's essential commitment to flexibility comes through as a business imperative. Indeed, the firm appointed its first woman to the top management team whose responsibilities include building the organization's workforce for the next century. Her highly visible task is to develop and evaluate the new career-development paths and service-delivery approaches that will shape PW's future workplace.

Flexible work arrangements are a business imperative. More and more frequently, as evidenced by Price Waterhouse and the Bank of Montreal, organizations achieve several business advantages when they adopt flex work practices. Paralleling society's changing demographics and expectations about leading a more balanced life, companies find that allowing employees to direct some of their work—where, when and how they get the job done—not only yields benefits in productivity and retention, but in customer responsiveness as well. By applying technology and many of the changes that already have occurred in the current workplace, they find satisfied, productive, efficient employees translate into revenue. ∎

Charlene Marmer Solomon is a contributing editor to PERSONNEL JOURNAL.

#2643

By Samuel Greengard

MAKING THE VIRTUAL OFFICE A REALITY

In an increasing number of companies, traditional office space is giving way to community areas and empty chairs as employees work from home, from their cars or from virtually anywhere. Advanced technologies and progressive HR strategies make these alternative offices possible.

It's 2 o'clock on a Wednesday afternoon. Inside the dining room of Chiat Day Mojo's Venice, California, offices, Nancy Alley, manager of HR, is downing a sandwich and soda while wading through phone and E-mail messages. In front of her a computer—equipped with a fax-modem—is plugged into a special port on the dining table. The contents of her briefcase are spread on the table. As she sifts through a stack of paperwork and types responses into the computer, she periodically picks up a cordless phone and places a call to a colleague or associate. As she talks, she sometimes wanders across the room.

To be sure, this isn't your ordinary corporate environment. Alley doesn't have a permanent desk or workspace, nor her own telephone. When she enters the ad agency's building, she checks out a portable Macintosh computer and a cordless phone and heads off to whatever nook or cranny she chooses. It might be the company library, or a common area under a bright window. It could even be the dining room or *Student Union*, which houses punching bags, televisions and a pool table. Wherever she goes, a *concierge* forwards mail and phone pages to her and a computer routes calls, faxes and E-mail messages to her assigned extension. She simply logs onto the firm's computer system and accesses her security-protected files.

"I'm not tethered to a specific work area; I'm not forced to function in any predefined way," says Alley, who spends mornings, and even sometimes an entire day, connected from home via sophisticated voicemail and E-mail systems, as well as a pager. "My work is process- and task-oriented. As long as I get everything done, that's what counts. Ultimately, my productivity is greater and my job-satisfaction level is higher. And for somebody trying to get in touch with me, it's seamless. Nobody can tell that I might be in my car or sitting at home reading a stack of resumes in my pajamas. The call gets forwarded to me wherever I'm working."

You've just entered the vast frontier of the virtual office—a universe in which leading-edge technology and new concepts redefine work and job functions by enabling employees to work from virtually anywhere. The concept allows a growing number of companies to alter their workplaces in ways never considered just a few years ago. They're scrapping assigned desks and conventional office space to create a bold new world where employees telecommute, function on a mobile basis or use satellite offices or communal work areas that are free of assigned spaces with personal paraphernalia.

IBM, AT&T, Travelers Corporation, Pacific Bell, Panasonic, Apple Computer and J.C. Penney are among the firms embracing the virtual-office concept. But they're just a few. The percentage of U.S. companies that have work-at-home programs alone has more than doubled in the past five years, from 7% in 1988 to 18% today. In fact, New York-based Link Resources, which tracks telecommuting and virtual-office trends, has found that 7.6 million Americans now telecommute—a figure that's expected to swell to 25 million by the year 2000. And if you add mobile workers—those who use their cars, client offices, hotels and satellite work areas to get the job done—there's an estimated 1 million more *virtual workers*.

Both companies and employees are discovering the benefits of virtual arrangements. Businesses that successfully incorporate them are able to slash real-estate costs and adhere to stringent air-quality regulations by curtailing traffic and commuters. They're also finding that by being flexible, they're more responsive to customers, while retaining key personnel who otherwise might be lost to a cross-country move or a newborn baby. And employees who successfully embrace the concept are better able to manage their work and personal lives. Left for the most part to work on their own terms, they're often happier, as well as more creative and productive.

Of course, the basic idea of working away from the office is nothing new. But today, high-speed notebook computers, lightning-fast data modems, telephone lines that provide advanced data-transmission capabilities, portable printers and wireless communication are fueling a quiet revolution. "As a society, we're transforming the way we work and what's possible," says Franklin Becker, director of the International Workplace Studies Program at Cornell University and a leading expert on the virtual office. "It's creating tremendous opportunities, but it also is generating a

great deal of stress and difficulty. There are tremendous organizational changes required to make it work."

Adds Loree Goffigon, a consultant at Santa Monica, California-based Hellmuth, Obata & Kassabaum (HOK), which helps companies implement alternative office strategies: "As markets have changed—as companies have downsized, streamlined and restructured—many have been forced to explore new ways to support the work effort. The virtual office, or alternative office, is one of the most effective strategies for dealing with these changes."

Of course, the effect of alternative officing on the HR function truly is great. HR must change the way it hires, evaluates employees and terminates them. It must train an existing work force to fit into a

new corporate paradigm. There are issues involving benefits, compensation and liability. And, perhaps most importantly, there's the enormous challenge of holding the corporate culture together—even if employees no longer spend time socializing over the watercooler or in face-to-face meetings. Notes Goffigon: "When a company makes a commitment to adopt a virtual-office environment—whether it's shared work-space or basic telecommuting—it takes time for people to acclimate and adjust. If HR can't meet the challenge, and employees don't buy in, then the program is destined to fail."

Virtual offices break down traditional office walls. Step inside Chiat Day and you quickly see how different an

Telecommuting Centers Provide an Alternative to the Corporate Office

In today's highly mobile environment, many companies are discovering that conventional corporate offices no longer fit the bill. They're expensive to maintain, and they're inconvenient for telecommuters and road warriors, who find themselves spending hours driving to and from a far-flung location. As a result, many firms now are turning to smaller telecommuting centers—places that offer a full-fledged office in a convenient location. At these sites, an employee can receive secretarial aid, make photocopies and pick up mail one or two days a week. Quite simply, they can step into a corporate environment that's equipped for their specific needs.

It may be the next great wave in alternative work environments. Already, a growing number of companies—including Pacific Bell and Panasonic—are creating their own satellite offices, and independent firms now are beginning to create shared telecommuting centers to cater to the growing demand. In Valencia, California, located ap-proximately 35 miles from downtown Los Angeles, the Newhall Land and Farming Company has created a prototype for corporate America. The 30,000-square-foot facility—a converted

warehouse—is equipped with state-of-the-art offices, conference rooms, free parking and convenient freeway access. Companies—including CareAmerica, Cigna and Great West-ern Savings—have already leased space.

"The center provides a place for telecommuters and others to work in their own community," says Jim Backer, director of marketing for commercial and industrial real estate at Newhall Land and Farming. "People find they no longer have to spend hours on the freeway getting to and from the office. It has improved their productivity and the quality of their lives."

Newhall Land and Farming has gone to great lengths to satisfy companies seeking space. All office suites are separate and secure. Furnished and unfurnished offices are available. And the overall environment has been designed and laid out by consultants who specialize in alternative worksites and tech-nology issues. To be sure, nothing is left to chance.

So far, the center has proven an overwhelming success. Not even a year after it opened the facility, Newhall Land and Farming is leasing at 100% occupancy.

And some of the firms—such as Chatsworth, California-based CareAmerica Health Plan Inc.—have discovered an array of supplemental benefits. During last January's earthquake, for example, the HMO provider used the site for recovery and emergency operations. Using computers, phones, mo-dems and faxes, personnel were able to keep the company online during trying times. Afterwards, commuters, who were cut off from their usual worksites by impassable roads and freeways, were able to set up shop and continue with minimal disruption.

Consultants such as Santa Monica, California-based Hellmuth, Obata & Kassabaum's Lor-ee Goffigon, believe that independent telecommuting centers soon may appear at airports and a variety of other locations. "The problem with a lot of business centers is that they're ugly and low-tech," says Goffigon. "By fashioning the concept for the '90s and providing cutting-edge capabilities, non-traditional workers have far more options available. Ultimately, that benefits them and the company."

—SG

environment the ad agency has created. Gone are the cubicles in which employees used to work. In their place are informal work carrels and open areas where any employee—whether it's Chairman Jay Chiat or an administrative assistant—can set up shop. Teams may assemble and disperse at any given spot, and meetings and conferences happen informally wherever it's convenient. Only a handful of maintenance workers, phone operators and food-services personnel, whose flexibility is limited by their particular jobs, retain any semblance of a private workspace.

Equally significant is the fact that on any given hour of any day, as many as one-third of the salaried work force aren't in the office. Some are likely working at a client's site, others at home or in a hotel room on the road. "The feeling," says Adelaid Horton, the firm's managing director of operations, "is that the employees of Chiat Day are self-starters. To empower the work force, we felt we could dispense with traditional structure and discipline. The work environment was designed around the concept that one's best thinking isn't necessarily done at a desk or in an office. Sometimes, it's done in a conference room with several people. Other times it's done on a ski slope or driving to a client's office. We wanted to eliminate the boundaries about where people are supposed to think. We wanted to create an environment that was stimulating and rich in resources." As such, employees decide on their own where they will work each day, and are judged on work produced rather than on hours put in at the office.

Another company that has jumped headfirst into the virtual-office concept is Armonk, New York-based International Business Machine's Midwest division. The regional business launched a virtual-office work model in the spring of 1993 and expects 2,500 of its 4,000 employees—sal-aried staff from sales, marketing, technical and customer service, including managers—to be mobile by the beginning of 1995. Its road warriors, equip-ped with IBM Think Pad computers, fax-modems, E-mail, cellular phones and a combination of proprietary and off-the-shelf software, use their cars, client offices and homes as work stations. When they do need to come into an office—usually once or twice a week—they log onto a computer that auto-matically routes calls and faxes to the desk at which they choose to sit.

So far, the program has allowed Big Blue's Midwest division to reduce real-estate space by nearly 55%, while increasing the ratio of employees to workstations from 4-to-1 to almost 10-to-1. More importantly, it has allowed the company to harness technology that allows employees to better serve customers and has raised the job-satisfaction level of workers. A recent survey indicated that 83% of the region's mobile work force wouldn't want to return to a traditional office environment.

IBM maintains links with the mobile work force in a variety of ways, says John F. Frank, project manager for mobility. All employees access their E-mail and voicemail daily; important messages and policy updates are broadcast regularly into the mailboxes of thousands of workers. When the need for teleconferencing arises, it can put hundreds of employees on the line simultaneously. Typically, the organization's mobile workers link from cars, home offices, hotels, even airplanes.

Virtual workers are only a phone call away. To be certain, *telephony* has become a powerful driver in the virtual-office boom. Satellites and high-tech telephone systems, such as ISDN phone lines, allow companies to zap data from one location to another at light speed. Organizations link to their work force and hold virtual meetings using tools such as videoconferencing. Firms grab a strategic edge in the marketplace by providing workers with powerful tools to access information.

Consider Gemini Consulting, a Morristown, New Jersey-based firm that has 1,600 employees spread throughout the United States and beyond. A sophisticated E-mail system allows employees anywhere to access a central bulletin board and data base via a toll-free phone number. Using Macintosh Powerbook computers and modems, they tap into electronic versions of The Associated Press, Reuters and *The Wall Street Journal*, and obtain late-breaking news and information on clients, key subjects, even executives within client companies. And that's just the beginning. Many of the firm's consultants have Internet addresses, and HR soon will begin training its officeless work force via CD-ROM. It will mail disks to workers, who will learn on their own schedule using machines the firm provides. The bottom line of this technology? Gemini can eliminate the high cost of flying consultants into a central location for training.

"Today, the technology exists to break the chains of traditional thought and the typical way of doing things," says Gordon Stone, senior vice president for Gemini. "It's possible to process information and knowledge in dramatically different ways than in the past." That can mean that instead of one individual or a group handling a project from start to finish, teams can process bits and pieces. They can assemble and disassemble quickly and efficiently.

Some companies, such as San Francisco-based Pacific Bell, have discovered that providing telecommuters with satellite offices can further facilitate efficiency. The telecommunications giant currently has nearly 2,000 managers splitting time bet-ween home and any of the company's of-fices spread throughout California. Those who travel regularly or prefer not to work at home also can drop into dozens of satellite facilities that each are equipped with a handful of workstations. At these centers, they can access proprietary data bases, check E-mail and make phone calls.

Other firms have pushed the telecommuting concept even further. One of them is Great Plains Software, a Fargo, North Dakota-based company that produces and markets PC-based accounting programs. Despite its remote—some might say undesirable—location, the company retains top talent by being flexible and innovative. Some of its high-level managers live and work in such places as Montana and New Jersey. Even its local employees

> It takes time for people to acclimate to a virtual-office environment. If HR can't meet the challenge, and employees don't buy in, the program is destined to fail.

may work at home a few days a week.

Lynne Stockstad's situation at Great Plains demonstrates how a program that allows for flexible work sites can benefit both employer and worker. The competitive-research specialist had spent two years at Great Plains when her husband decided to attend chiropractic college in Davenport, Iowa. At most firms, that would have prompted Stockstad to resign—something that also would have cost the company an essential employee. Instead, Stockstad and Great Plains devised a system that would allow her to telecommute from Iowa and come to Fargo only for meetings when absolutely necessary. Using phone, E-mail, voicemail and fax, she and her work team soon found they were able to link together, and complete work just as efficiently as before. Today, with her husband a recent graduate, Stockstad has moved back to Fargo and has received a promotion.

Great Plains uses similar technology in other innovative ways to build a competitive advantage. For example, it has developed a virtual hiring process. Managers who are spread across the country conduct independent interviews with candidates, and then feed their responses into the company's computer. Later, the hiring team holds a meeting, usually via phone or videoconferencing, to render a verdict. Only then does the firm fly the candidate to Fargo for the final interview.

"The virtual office radically changes thinking. It totally changes the corporate culture," notes Cornell's Becker. "Although many companies are attracted to the cost savings—real estate, maintenance, security, landscaping, energy and insurance can all be cut—many discover it has a lot of other benefits. It's forcing organizations to fundamentally rethink how they function."

HR must lay the infrastructure to support a mobile work force. Just as a cafeteria offers a variety of foods to suit individual taste and preferences, the workplace of the future is evolving toward a model for which alternative work options likely will become the norm. "Nobody says you have to work the same way, even if you have the same job," says Becker. "One person may find that telecommuting four days a week is great; another may find that he or she functions better in the

office. The common denominator for the organization is: How can we create an environment in which people are able to produce to their maximum capabilities?"

Creating such a model and making it work is no easy task, however. Such a shift in resources requires a fundamental change in thinking. And it usually falls squarely on HR's shoulders to oversee the program and hold the organization together during trying times. "When a company decides to participate in an alternative officing program, people need to acclimate and adjust to the new etiquette," says HOK's Goffigon. "Workers are used to doing things a certain way. Suddenly, their world is being turned upside down."

From an HR perspective, one of the biggest problems is laying the infrastructure to support such a system. Often, it's necessary to tweak benefits and compensation, create new job descriptions and methods of evaluation and find innovative ways to communicate. Sometimes, be-cause companies are liable for their workers while they're "on the clock," HR must send inspectors to home offices to ensure they're safe.

When Great Plains Software started its telecommuting program in the late 1980s, it established loose guidelines for employees who wanted to be involved in the program. "We pretty much implemented policies on an unscientific basis," says Lynn Dreyer, director of HR for the company. Over time, the company has evolved to a far more stringent system of determining who qualifies and how the job is defined.

For example, as with most other companies that embrace the virtual-office concept, Great Plains stipulates that only salaried employees can work in virtual offices because of the lack of a structured time schedule and the potential for working more than eight hours a day. Those employees who want to telecommute must first articulate how the decision will benefit the company, the department and themselves. Only those who can convince a hiring manager that they meet all three

criteria move on to the next stage.

Potential telecommuters then must define how they'll be accountable and responsible in the new working model. "We ask them to specify their performance expectations—particularly in communication," notes Dreyer. "The last thing you want is someone feeling like an outside consultant rather than part of the company."

Finally, once performance standards and guidelines have been created, Great Plains presents two disclaimers to those going virtual. "We tell them that if their performance falls below certain predetermined standards, we'll review the situation to determine whether it's working. And if the position changes significantly and it no longer makes sense to telecommute, we will have to reevaluate," says Dreyer. She explains that early on, some workers assumed the arrangement would be permanent and were taken aback when changes warranted ending it. "We learned that you can't create the assumption that this is a lifetime program," she says.

Other companies have adopted similar checks and balances. "We're training HR advisers to make accommodations for the individual, but to not make accommodations for the person's job responsibilities," says Frank. "[But] we don't want to create artificial safety nets that make it easy to go back to traditional ways of working. Otherwise, the program is doomed to failure."

IBM provides counseling from behavioral scientists and offers ongoing assistance to those having trouble adapting to the new work model. By closely monitoring preestablished sales and productivity benchmarks, managers quickly can determine if there's a problem. So far, Frank says only approximately 10% to 15% of its mobile work force has required counseling, and only a handful of employees have had to be reassigned.

Virtual workers need guidance from HR. Not everyone is suited to working in a virtual-office environment.

> **Just as a cafeteria offers a variety of foods to suit individual tastes, the workplace is evolving toward a model for which alternative work options will be the norm.**

Not only must workers who go mobile or work at home learn to use the technology effectively, but they also must adjust their workstyle and lifestyle. Says Cornell's Becker: "The more you get connected, the harder it is to disconnect. At some point, the boundaries between work and personal life blur. Without a good deal of discipline, the situation can create a lot of stress."

Managers often fear that employees will not get enough work done if they can't see them. Most veterans of the virtual office, however, maintain that the exact opposite is true. All too often, employees wind up fielding phone calls in the evening or stacking an extra hour or two on top of an eight-hour day. Not surprisingly, that can create an array of problems, including burnout, errors and marital discord.

IBM learned early on that it has to teach employees to remain in control of the technology and not let it overrun their lives. One of the ways it achieves the goal is to provide its mobile work force with two-line telephones. That way, employees can recognize calls from work, switch the ringer off at the end of the workday and let the voicemail system pick up calls.

Another potential problem with which virtual employees must deal is handling all the distractions that can occur at home. As a result, many firms provide workers with specific guidelines for handling work at home. "It's essential to give the company one's full effort," says Great Plains' Dreyer. "We expect that those who work at home will arrange child care or elder care." And although she recognizes there are times when a babysitter falls through or a problem occurs, "If someone's surrounded by noisy children, it creates an impression that the individual isn't working or is distracted."

Still, most say that problems aren't common. "The majority of workers adjust and become highly productive in an alternative office environment," says HOK's Goffigon. "The most important thing for a company to do is lay out guidelines and suggestions that help workers adapt."

At many firms, including IBM, HR now is providing booklets that cover a range of topics, including time management and family issues. Many companies also send out regular mailings that not only provide tips and work strategies but also keep employees informed of company events and keep them ingrained in the cor-

Lynn Dreyer
Great Plains Software

We ask telecommuters to specify their performance plans—particularly in communication. The last thing you want is someone not feeling a part of the company.

porate culture.

This type of correspondence also helps alleviate workers' fears of isolation. IBM goes one step further by providing voluntary outings, such as to the Indianapolis 500, for its mobile work force. Even without these events, however, virtual workers' isolation fears often are unfounded. "The level of interaction in a virtual office actually can be heightened and intensified," says Becker. "Because workers aren't in the same place every day, they may be exposed to a wider range of people and situations. And that can open their eyes and minds to new ideas and concepts."

However, dismantling the traditional office structure can present other HR challenges. One of the most nettlesome can be dealing with issues of identity and status. Workers who've toiled for years to earn a corner office suddenly can find themselves thrown into a ubiquitous work pod. Likewise, photographs and other personal items often must disappear as workspace is shared. But solutions do exist. For in-

stance, when IBM went mobile, top executives led by example. They immediately cleared out their desks and began plugging in at common work pods.

Not surprisingly, one of the most difficult elements in creating a virtual office is dealing with this human side of the equation. Indeed, the human factor can send shock waves reverberating through even the most staid organization. "When all the accessories are stripped away, a company must redefine its success indicators," says Goffigon. "They're saying they don't just value people sitting at their desk, they value results. Suddenly, there's a huge paradigm shift in the workers' heads. It's a tremendous challenge for HR."

According to Goffigon, this challenge requires HR to become a proactive business partner. That means working with other departments, such as real estate, finance and information technology. It means creating the tools to make a virtual office work. In some cases, that may require HR to completely rewrite a benefits package to include a $500- or $1,000-a-month stipend for those working at home. That way, the company saves money on real-estate and relocation costs, while the employee receives an incentive that can be used to furnish a home office.

HR also must change the way supervisors evaluate their workers. Managers easily can fall into the trap of thinking that only face-to-face interaction is meaningful and may pass over mobile workers for promotions. Great Plains has gone to great lengths to ensure that its performance-evaluation system functions in a virtual environment. The company asks its managers to conduct informal reviews quarterly with telecommuting employees, and formal reviews every six months. By increasing the interaction and dialogue, the company has eliminated much of the anxiety for employees—and their managers—while providing a better gauge of performance. In the final analysis, the system no longer measures good citizenship and attendance, but how much work people actually get done and how well they do it.

Adds Becker: "Today, the odds that a manager will find a specific employee at a desk on the spur of the moment isn't always so great. People now have more channels of communication then at any time in the past. Face-to-face interaction is less important than ever before."

Still, many experts point out that too much reliance on voicemail and E-mail can present problems. Although instantaneous messaging is convenient and efficient, it can overload virtual workers with too much information and not enough substance. "It isn't what you communicate, it's how you communicate. Without some human interaction it's impossible to build relationships and a sense of trust within an organization," Dreyer points out.

Sending workers offsite can boost productivity, while saving costs. Those who have embraced the virtual office say that it's a concept that works. At Pacific Bell, which began experimenting with telecommuting during the 1984 Summer Olympics in Los Angeles, employees routinely have reported 100%

increases in productivity. Equally important: "They tell us that this fits into family and flexibility issues and that they enjoy working for the company more than ever before," says Gary Fraundorfer, manager of HR quality communications strategy.

Emily Brassman, the company's director of virtual office development, plunged into the lifestyle with unwavering commitment. She now spends three to four days a week at home, and schedules face-to-face meetings all on the same days. Using a notebook computer, portable printer and a separate business line in her home, she's in constant touch with the office. "In most cases, nobody has any idea where I'm working. It's completely invisible to them."

Although the final results aren't yet in, IBM's mobile work force reports a 10% boost in morale and appears to be processing more work, more efficiently. What's

more, its customers have so far reported highly favorable results, says Andre'a Cheatham, manager of the National Mobility Project. "People are happier and more productive because they can have breakfast with their family before they go off to client meetings. They can go home and watch their child's soccer game and then do work in the evening. They no longer are bound by a nine-to-five schedule. The only criterium is that they meet results."

And at Chiat Day, the outcome speaks for itself. After the Los Angeles earthquake in January, the organization used virtual-office technology to link work teams and keep operations running at full speed. Now, long after the disaster, employees adhere to their own timetables and work preferences. "There's a fundamental change in philosophy," says Horton. There's a focus on quality and not physi-

Traditional Labor Laws Apply to the Non-traditional Office

BY PATRICK MCCARTHY

At-home work can confer many benefits to all involved and is an excellent solution for many work situations. However, it also can give rise to potential problems in complying with wage-and-hour laws and health-and-safety regulations.

The Department of Labor takes the position that an employer that "suffers or permits" an employee to work more than 40 hours in a week must pay overtime. That can be true even if employers don't authorize the overtime and make it clear to at-home workers that their job is listed for straight time only. Usually enforcement agencies hold that if there's no proof to the contrary, whatever the employee claims is sufficient proof to warrant a judgment for back pay and penalties. And, workers have as long as two—and in some cases three—years to claim these wages.

To reduce the likelihood of wage-and-hour claims by at-home workers, employers should:

1) Establish and enforce methods for monitoring work done at home. Keep accurate records proving what hours are worked. This can be done by having a verifiable system for employees to self-report or certify in writing the hours they

work each week, and by maintaining a paper trail to make sure employees can't come back later and claim they've worked additional hours.

2) Educate operating managers and supervisors about the necessity for keeping workers within the 40-hour workweek. Employers need to ensure that supervisors don't tell their workers to "get the work done regardless of the time it takes," or "process 75 claims each day" without considering that assignments may take longer for certain workers.

3) Use such technology as time clocks, or other equipment that records hours. Time expended on behalf of the employer for preliminary and follow-up work should be counted as well.

4) Give employees explicit written directions not to work more than 40 hours without prior written supervisory approval. Check with them to ascertain that they're not doing so.

Health-and-safety law compliance presents another set of problems. There's often the same potential in an at-home office for injuries resulting from repetitive motion, use of hazardous chemicals or lifting as in the traditional workplace. And, because these injuries occur without the

witnesses that may be present in a traditional office, workers' compensation claims are more difficult to police. The situation is ripe for fraudulent claims.

Minimal steps should be taken to combat this problem, including imposing strict reporting requirements. Require that all injuries be reported immediately, and request specific information about how the injury occured and what the symptoms are to make verification easier.

Lastly, employees and their employers need to watch out for exposure to third-party injury claims. At-home workers' negligence and intentional acts while employed can make employers liable for damages. Most, if not all, problems can be minimized with proper forethought. Identification of risks and planning to maximize compliance are a must. These usually are areas of responsibility for HR managers. Therefore, companies planning telecommuting programs should ensure that HR considerations don't lag behind the technological focus of such change.

Patrick McCarthy is a partner in the labor/employment law department of Pitney, Hardin, Kipp & Szuch, a Morristown, New Jersey law firm.

VIRTUAL OFFICES

cally being someplace."

In the end, says Becker, HR must become a major player in the transformation and keep both management and workers on track. "There's a need to support people through all the changes," he says. "And that requires mechanisms to encourage discussion and ways to solve problems. Migrating to a virtual office can be a positive and rewarding experience—but only if all the pieces are firmly in place."

HOK's Goffigon says that she believes society is on the frontier of a fundamental change in the way the workplace is viewed and how work is handled. "In the future, it will become increasingly difficult for traditional companies to compete against those embracing the virtual office," she says. "Companies that embrace the concept are sending out a loud message. They're mak-

ing it clear that they're interested in their employees' welfare, that they're seeking a competitive edge, and that they aren't afraid to rethink—even reengineer—their work force for changing conditions. Those are the ingredients for future success." ∎

Samuel Greengard is a free-lance writer based in Los Angeles.

The Pros and Cons of Alternative Office Strategies

Companies that employ alternative office strategies—from providing shared workspace for a number of employees to equipping roaming workers with cellular phones and portable computers—can unleash their employees' creativity, boost productivity and cut costs. But, they also can create conflict, worker disconnection and management problems. Below are descriptions of the different strategies being employed, along with the pros and cons of each.

Type of Strategy	Organizational and Individual Advantages and Benefits	Organizational and Individual Disadvantages and Pitfalls
Shared Space: two or more employees share a single, assigned workspace	• Better use of space • Can increase headcount without increasing space required	• Employees may be reluctant to give up own space • Requires employees to work closely with one another, and maintain files and work area in an orderly manner
Group Address: a designated group or team space for a specified period of time	• Project team orientation of users ensures high, ongoing utilization rate • Encourages interaction between team members	• Size of teams may create space shortage • Turnover of spaces among users is difficult to manage • Requires accurate projections of user size and volume
Activity Settings: a variety of work settings to fit diverse individual or group activities	• Provides users with a choice of setting that best responds to tasks • Fosters team interaction	• Requires advanced technological equipment • File retrieval can be problematic
Free Address: a workspace shared on a first-come, first-serve basis	• Maximizes use of unassigned space • Minimizes real-estate overhead • Minimizes cost of workstations and office construction • Suitable for sales and consultant practices	• Access to files and storage can be problematic • Probability is high for scheduling conflicts • Probably requires a substantial investment in equipment and training
Hoteling: employees reserve workspace	• Accommodates staff increases without increase in facilities and leasing costs • Can result in upgrade in office amenities	• Storage can be problematic • Probability is high for scheduling conflicts
Satellite Offices: office centers used full time by employees closest to them	• Lowers rentable costs per square foot • Reduces communication time	• Remote management is a challenge • Employees may feel disconnected from the organization • May impede ease of inter-office communication
Telecommuting: using a combination of home and office workspace	• Reduces transportation and real-estate costs • Can improve quality of personal life • Can increase productivity	• Home-office equipment may be inadequate • Reduces staff interaction • Home-office space may not be quiet and free from interruptions
Remote Telecenters: office centers located away from the main office, close to clients; workers can access technology and support	• Achieves clean-air act mandates • Fosters productivity and employee loyalty through improved family life	• Requires clear guidelines and supervisory support
Virtual Office: the freedom to office anywhere, supported by technology	• Can increase employee productivity • May increase time with clients due to reduced commute time • Reduces space and attendant occupancy costs	• May impact employee connection to the organization • Requires new criteria for evaluating performance • Reduces employee interaction

Source: The HOK Facilities Consulting Report reproduced by permission only. For more information, contact Loree Goffigon, 310/453-0100.

MORE THAN 9.2 MILLION AMERICANS TELECOMMUTE, A

NUMBER EXPECTED TO TRIPLE IN THE NEXT 15 YEARS.

Making Telecommuting

HERE ARE THE PROS AND CONS OF TELECOMMUTING AND A

DESCRIPTION OF A TRAINING PROGRAM TO GET PEOPLE READY TO

TELECOMMUTE, PLUS TIPS ON SETTING UP AN OFFICE AT HOME.

It's Monday morning and the start of a new workweek.

▶ In New York City, the HR executive committee of a large telecommunications firm is discussing how they will comply with revisions of the 1990 Federal Clean Air Act which require decreased employee commuting for all companies with over 100 employees.

▶ In California, a mid-sized, high-tech company is developing its own

BY GEORGE M. PISKURICH

Illustration by Dave Plunkert

Work

compliance plans for that state's even tougher air quality standards which mandate a reduction in employee trips to work.

 ▶ In Atlanta, a fast-growing company is concerned about the cost and availability of new office space.

 ▶ And in Chicago, another HR department listens to complaints from employees about traffic jams caused by freeway repairs and criticism from their supervisors about tardiness and decreased productivity.

Why telecommuting?
What these and many other companies with similar problems have in common is that they are all exploring telecommuting as a possible solution. They see telecommuting as a way to help them meet government air pollution regulations, comply with ADA accommodation requirements, reduce operating costs by decreasing office space, and increase employee satisfaction by eliminating long commutes. As a by-product they also expect increased productivity from employees who aren't exhausted from fighting traffic, leaving early to "beat the rush," and who are working when their bio-clocks make them most effective.

Organizations seeking a competitive advantage in everything from better customer service to reduced turnover are considering and, in many cases, trying telecommuting. In recent surveys, 60 to 70 percent of the companies polled offer or plan to offer some type of telecommuting option to their employees. In the communications field that number is 80 percent, and in higher education 90 percent.

The actual number of telecommuters is hard to determine because defining what constitutes a telecommuter is problematic. Some surveys suggest that there are more than 7 million telecommuters in the United States, with 750,000 in California alone. This number does not include people who are self-employed and work at home. These individuals are not considered telecommuters as they normally have no other office to be telecommuting from.

While the number of telecommuters comprises less than 2 percent of the workforce, it is growing, possibly as much as 15 percent a year. One multinational communications organization has announced a goal of having 20,000 telecommuters in place by the end of the decade. Estimates of 11 to 15 million telecommuters by the

year 2000 may actually be conservative as more and more companies of all sizes begin to realize the benefits of telecommuting.

Advantages and disadvantages
Some of the benefits of telecommuting have already been mentioned. A more comprehensive, though by no means exhaustive, list is provided in the box on this page. This list has been divided into business, employee, and community advantages, though some obviously overlap.

These advantages also translate into real dollars. The average office space savings per telecommuting worker can be as high as $8,000. Companies are saving two dollars for every dollar invested in telecommuting. One company documented a savings of $80 million in 1994, simply in office rentals.

In terms of productivity, studies suggest that telecommuters can outperform in-office workers by as much as 16 percent. A significant portion of this gain is from being able to custom design a work schedule. Telecommuters who are morning people don't waste their most productive hours trying to get to the office. And those who are evening people don't need to leave for home just as their productive time is beginning.

Another reason for increased productivity is fewer interruptions from telephones, meetings, and colleagues.

Some telecommuting advantages can be a two-edged sword. For example, fewer people in the office means less need for office space, but also less flexibility in a crisis. The box on page 23 lists disadvantages of telecommuting. A number of these disadvantages are the flip side of the advantages, and proper implementation can significantly decrease or eliminate their effects.

Misconceptions about telecommuting are a major disadvantage. Some employees regard it as a substitute for day-care services, or a chance to get away permanently from the office and its problems. Neither of these perceptions fits the reality of telecommuting.

Managers often believe that telecommuting will cause them to lose control of their employees, or will re-

TELECOMMUTING ADVANTAGES

For the company
Helps attract new employees, especially those who need flexibility
Can increase retention rates
Helps in ADA compliance
Complies with various EPA regulations
Reduces sick time and absenteeism
Increases productivity
Increases employee job satisfaction
Maximizes office space
Decreases relocation costs
Reduces overtime

For the employee
Reduces transportation costs and commuting time
Allows personal control over working conditions (temperature, music, etc.)
Eliminates unplanned (unproductive) meetings or "drop-ins"

Provides more flexible child and elder care options
Increases privacy
Reduces the stress of commuting
Allows work to be done when one is most productive
Reduces clothing costs
Creates more time to spend with family
Enhances communications with supervisor
Provides the ability to work without interruption

For the community
Decreases the environmental impact of commuting
Conserves energy
Decreases traffic congestion
Reduces the need for road repair
Takes pressure from public transportation

duce the need for managers. Many think that departmental communications will suffer, and that the employees will slack off.

In reality, telecommuting can increase the importance and responsibilities of good managers. It usually leads to better communications, and it consistently results in employees who work harder so they can keep their telecommuting option open. However, a decision to offer telecommuting should not be made without a thorough examination of how these misconceptions, and the other disadvantages as well, will affect the telecommuting program.

A review of advantages and disadvantages is only one step toward successful telecommuting. Many telecommuting programs fail because the decision to implement them seems so simple and logical that not enough time is spent planning them.

Defining telecommuting

One of the first and most critical decisions in planning a telecommuting initiative is to define what it means for the company. Definitions for telecommuting range from simply working at home to the more complicated combination of flexiplace, flexitime, and electronic communications.

Telecommuting may include aspects of other alternatives to traditional office arrangements. One definition of telecommuting may be based on job sharing, another on flexitime, a third on compressed workweeks, while a fourth combines all three. One thing that telecommuting is not, however, is a way to turn employees into independent contractors. Beyond the legal ramifications, a telecommuting initiative with this objective is almost certain to fail. A company that expects telecommuting to reduce employee benefits expenses will soon find itself with new problems, including some interesting discussions with the IRS.

All aspects of what might constitute telecommuting for a company need to be considered before a definition can be determined and agreed upon. The definition is the cornerstone of the telecommuting initiative, so it should be detailed enough to provide the boundaries of the telecommuting

■ Many telecommuting programs fail due to a lack of planning ■

process. Don't make the mistake one company did by defining telecommuting as "not commuting."

Target populations

Another factor to consider during planning is the telecommuting target population. Is it large enough to give a return that warrants the time and energy that will be invested in the process? Companies have found that only 15 to 25 percent of those eligible will volunteer for telecommuting. Involuntary telecommuting is not something that any business should ever consider, except in dire circumstances.

Once a definition and a commitment to attempt telecommuting have been agreed upon, the next step is to develop the telecommuting policy and procedures that will guide the initiative. These policies and procedures should reflect the advantages that the company and the employee can expect to gain from telecommuting. They provide the framework for the specific processes within which the telecommuters and their managers will function. At a minimum, they should include the following:
▶ a statement of why the company supports telecommuting
▶ an agreed-upon definition of telecommuting for the company
▶ a list of the most important benefits of telecommuting for the employee, company, and community
▶ the criteria that will be used to se-

DISADVANTAGES OF TELECOMMUTING

For the company
Decreases direct control of employees
Reduces face-to-face supervisory meetings
May be abused by employees
Decreases corporate flexibility in emergency situations
Creates problems with off-site mechanical breakdowns
Demands greater coordination
May decrease the amount of communication
Is only suitable to certain jobs
May create psychological problems for the telecommuters

For the employees
May create a sense of loneliness and isolation
Can lead to cabin fever
May create a lack of respect or jealousy from fellow workers
Can lead to workaholism

Can provide distractions that interfere with work
Offers less access to copiers, fax, and other office services
May cause "invisibility" which can be bad for one's career
Creates mail handling problems (in both directions)
Diminishes participation in the office culture
Can create a sense of never getting away from the office
Creates situations where things you need have been left at the office
Eliminates the private office, and the feelings of comfort and status that come with it
Can produce higher household utility bills

For the community
Can lead to possible job and revenue losses

151

JOBS THAT TELECOMMUTE

Telecommuting has been attempted in almost any job that you can imagine. Most often it has been used in sales positions as sales people are used to not being in the office. However, because they spend so much time on the road many sales people find it particularly difficult to give up their "office nests" and become telecommuters.

Positions that require the use of a computer and telephone for a majority of their daily work come in second on the list. These jobs can range from data entry clerk to help desk specialist, and even customer service representative.

Some telemarketing companies have gone so far as to have their catalogue order numbers ring in employees' homes. No one ever seems to notice the difference, except for the employee who has a much more comfortable work environment. Many telecommuting customer service workers have noted that they are more responsive to customers' needs and feelings when stationed in their own homes.

Almost any job, computer-oriented or not, that doesn't demand the employee to be at an office location every day (in almost every well-conceived telecommuting initiative, the employee has some office days) is a candidate for telecommuting. Even managers and CEOs have been known to telecommute.

A telecommuting job should have activities that can be measured, be done for the most part independently, be portable to a non-office environment, have observable beginning and end points, not need special equipment that is only at the work site, and not have deadline requirements that come from outside the telecommuter's department.

Some positions, such as receptionist, won't work for telecommuting. However, jobs that don't require face-to-face interaction eight hours a day are possible candidates for telecommuting.

the primary cause of failure for most telecommuting initiatives.

Good communications and effective training that helps select and prepare the right people for telecommuting is paramount to the success of the process. Telecommuters who have not been well prepared can find themselves to be incompatible with telecommuting or frustrated by not being able to get what they need to do their work. They often become less rather than more productive. As an example, after the Los Angeles earthquake, the state of the freeway system caused Pacific Bell to initiate a telecommuting program. Later, most of the telecommuters voluntarily returned to the office. The main reason cited for their return was a lack of preparation and training.

A telecommuting training system

Effective telecommuting training can be divided into five components. While different in purpose, these components are closely related and usually developed simultaneously.

The first component is a communications program that introduces the process of telecommuting to the organization. This program can be as simple as a memo or as complex as a videotape production. One company found an audiotape that commuters listened to in their cars to be a particularly effective tool.

This introduction describes telecommuting based on the company's definition and telecommuting policy. It includes items such as:
‣ advantages for the company
‣ advantages for the employee
‣ positions within the company that are best for telecommuting (see box on this page)
‣ disadvantages
‣ common questions
‣ information on how to proceed if interested.

This program receives wide distribution; everyone in the telecommuting target population, their managers, and all higher-level administrators are possible recipients. It is particularly important that the latter two groups participate because their support will be critical to the success of the process.

lect possible telecommuters
‣ a list of what the telecommuter will be expected to do and not do in a work-at-home environment
‣ the administrative aspects of the program such as responsibility for telephone, office supplies, and household expenses
‣ HR issues that may differ in the telecommuting environment
‣ the types of equipment and software that will be necessary, and how they should be obtained
‣ how the home office should be set up to best support the employee and ensure company security
‣ miscellaneous information specific to the company's needs such as security, support services, and so forth
‣ information on what the employee and manager need to do to get the telecommuting process started.

The importance of training

At this point, the company's HRD department becomes crucial to the telecommuting process. Its responsi-

bility is to take the policies and procedures and translate them into a coordinated communications and training process that will pave the way for successful telecommuting.

Preferably, the HRD department will have been involved in the process from the beginning, when advantages are discussed, definitions created, and procedures written. This involvement will significantly shorten the program design time and create more effective training.

The pressure to begin realizing the benefits of telecommuting for the company and the employees is usually intense. This impatience to begin is often enhanced by space problems, leases running out, or other economic factors. When all of these factors are added to what often appears to be the simple process of having people work at home, it's easy to see how the communications and training aspects of a telecommuting implementation can be neglected or ignored. This neglect is

Suitability and commitment

A second training component, designed for those employees who have expressed an interest in telecommuting based on the introduction program, helps them explore the reality of telecommuting and their suitability for it.

A psychological profile is part of this process. It starts the participants thinking about what mental and emotional characteristics make a good telecommuter, and what their own comfort level might be in a telecommuting environment.

Some form of simulation that gives a taste of telecommuting is also important in this part of the training. This might be anything from a written simulation to actually networking the trainees on their computers and having them do such everyday telecommuting processes as calling in, checking voice and phone mail, and accessing and sharing files.

Another aspect of this phase of training is an in-depth discussion of telecommuting advantages and disadvantages for the participant. Items that should receive special emphasis here include: dealing with demands from relatives and neighbors while working at home, the importance of itemizing and setting deadlines on work to be delivered, staying in touch with co-workers, addressing concerns about the loss of office and workplace visibility, and managing career development.

Personal advantages and disadvantages should be recorded by each of the participants as a summary of information they will need to help them make their final decisions.

Another series of items that participants can record on this document are their personal strengths and weaknesses in relation to telecommuting. See the box on this page for some traits of successful telecommuters.

The final step in this part of the training is to have the participants express their commitment to telecommuting, if that is their decision. This is usually accomplished through some type of contract, and is best done with the telecommuter's supervisor present.

The contract or commitment states how the telecommuter plans to func-

TRAITS OF SUCCESSFUL TELECOMMUTERS

Successful telecommuters should be:
Good planners
Self-motivated
Strong communicators
Task-oriented
Able to manage their workload effectively
Aware of their personal work style preferences
Able to work among family members
Flexible
Not just looking for an escape from the office
Committed and responsible
Able to ask for feedback
"Doers," not procrastinators
Able to work independently, with minimal supervision
Able to work without continual input and support from others
As comfortable eating lunch alone as with "the gang"
Able to leave the work behind when it is time to end the day
Able to negotiate work time and prevent interruptions from family and friends
Able to miss office gossip
Realistic about what can and can't be done
Able to adapt readily to new situations
Trustworthy
Good time managers
Proven producers of quality work
Able to focus on priorities and meet deadlines

> ■ *Help your employees explore the reality of telecommuting* ■

tion in the telecommuting environment, and what support he or she will need from the supervisor and the rest of the office staff. It can be as simple or as complicated as the company and the individual feel is necessary. Items such as schedules of availability, office days, supervisory and office communications plans, and how phone and mail will be handled are often found in these documents.

The contract has three main purposes: to indicate that the individual is ready to commit to telecommuting, to set out the plan by which this will be accomplished, and to document who is responsible for what in this individual's telecommuting environment.

Manager training

A supervisor's support is critical to the success of the telecommuter. If a lack of proper training is the main reason that telecommuting initiatives fail, poorly prepared managers and supervisors run a very close second.

Managers need to believe in the effectiveness of telecommuting, and they must know how to implement and manage it correctly. More than 50 percent of the companies that responded to a recent survey indicated that the lack of management's understanding and involvement was the greatest detriment to successful telecommuting.

Because they are directly involved in the contract and commitment aspects of preparing telecommuters, managers and supervisors should receive their own telecommuting training well before this process takes place.

Telecommuter skills training

The fourth component of a telecommuting training program is designed for those who have made the commitment to become telecommuters. This might be labeled telecommuting skills training. The following areas need to be covered:

▶ Telecommuting policies and procedures: Here the details of how the company sees the telecommuting process working are discussed, and the contract revised to reflect procedural changes.

▶ Getting started: The how-tos of obtaining equipment, setting up a home office (including ergonomics, second phone lines, space, privacy, and safe-

TELECOMMUTING PREDICTIONS

This year 9.2 million Americans will telecommute, according to a recent study by Link Resources Corp., a number that experts say will triple within the next 15 years. In the October, 1995, issue of *Wired* magazine, the editors polled five experts to look at the future of telecommuting. Among their predictions:

▶ In order to minimize employee isolation and bureaucratic ineffectiveness, adapting to individual lifestyles will take a backseat to getting people out in the field to better respond to customers.

▶ A "virtual water cooler" may emerge with the advent of affordable desktop, full-motion videoconferencing.

▶ Especially in the world of finance where minutes can mean millions, hand-held telephones that allow for global roaming will proliferate.

▶ "Virtual corporations" will not be entirely virtual; physical real estate will still be required for meetings and communication centers and classroom space for training.

SETTING UP AN OFFICE AT HOME

Here's what you can expect to pay to set up a typical office at home.

Furnishings
Workstation: Computer table, desk, printer stand—$400 to $600
Chair—$100 to $300
Chair mat—$30
Lamp—$40
File cabinet, four-drawer—$200
Bookcase—$150
Desk accessories (stapler, tape dispenser, desk pad, in/outboxes, and so forth)—$80

Technology
Monitor: 17-inch—$800;
15-inch—$500
Main unit and keyboard: Pentium—$2500; 486—$1900;
16Mb RAM, CD-ROM, 14.4 modem,
Macintosh—$2400,includes monitor

Mouse pad—$7
Printer-laser b&w—$800;
color—$600; b&w—$400
Software—$495 (negotiate for an upgrade with a dealer)
Disk drawers/holders—$30
Surge protector—$50
Phone: two-line, conferencing—$80
Answering machine—$50
Fax machine: plain paper—$650;
regular—$300
Extra phone lines: data—$22 installation, $200 per month;
Voice—$70 installation, $17 per month, plus a per-call charge.

Reminder
Make sure your work space has enough electrical outlets with sufficient current.

By: Carol Brown, ASTD staff

ty requirements), getting on the company network, and starting phone and voice mail, are described.

▶ Computer brush-up: Most telecommuters will need to use computers and should be computer literate, and this is where any special tricks or necessities are covered. Everyone is either brought up to the minimum level that will support telecommuting, or is recommended for additional training.

▶ New software: Often there will be new software needed for the telecommuting process, particularly in the areas of networking and communications. Information on how to use it, or resources on where to go to learn, are given.

▶ Other hardware: Beyond computers there is certainly a need for phones, and possibly for fax machines, scanners, copiers, shredders, surge protectors, and other equipment. Need, set up, and use are discussed here.

▶ Support: Where and how to get it

and what to expect are discussed.

With this training completed, the participant is now ready to begin telecommuting. All that seemingly remains is to set up the home office and get started. However, there is one more aspect to a good implementation.

Non-telecommuter training
Often overlooked, with disastrous results, is the training of employees who are not telecommuting. As they form the basic support structure for the telecommuter, their understanding and support are extremely important. This is basically a communications process, and is often best handled by a well-prepared supervisor in a group meeting attended by both the telecommuters and their in-the-office colleagues.

Some of the topics to be covered were addressed in the introduction to the telecommuting program, and simply need to be restated if everyone in the group attended. Other topics will be very specific to each individual work group and supervisor. It is important to the success of the initiative that the telecommuters not be left out on their own. This part of the training, plus follow-up group discussions on how the process is working, will help ensure that this does not happen.

Telecommuting problems
Even with proper preparation and training, problems will still arise during telecommuting implementation and with individual telecommuters. At the very least, there are possible problem areas that need to be monitored. These include:

Home-office problems: These might include a greater need for work space than was first predicted, feelings of isolation or cabin fever, non-work disruptions, and the inability of the telecommuter to discipline him- or herself to work effectively .

In-office problems: Includes the forwarding of office mail, receiving phone messages, and availability of desk space on office days.

Supervisor/telecommuter communications problems: Too little, too much, or the wrong kind of communication between a telecommuter and supervisor can all cause difficulties.

Invisibility problems: This can include

missing office parties or not even being sent an invitation to them, not being available for impromptu meetings, lack of consideration for special assignments, and generally not being part of the everyday flow of the office, from gossip to work-related discussions with colleagues.

Jealousy: Some employees who don't telecommute may feel that the telecommuters are not working, or, at least, not pulling their fair share at home.

Guilt: There are telecommuters who deep down are not sure that working without putting on business clothes and going to an office is really working, or who feel guilty about not having to commute to work.

Lost office and status: The lack of a personal and personalized office and the status that comes from doors, windows, and other symbols can affect a telecommuter, particularly when he or she must work in a shared cubical on in-office days. The belief that being on the fast track, or having access to the boss are not possible for telecommuters can undermine the telecommuters' sense of well-being.

In the final analysis, telecommuting is not the simple panacea for thorny business problems that many organizations envision. It is, however, a work strategy that can increase productivity and decrease overhead costs for large and small companies, while helping reduce air pollution and creating a healthier environment for everyone. With careful planning, good training, and conscientious monitoring, telecommuting can be effective. ∎

George M. Piskurich is an independent consultant. He can be reached at 102 Fernwood Court, Chapel Hill, NC 27516; 919/968-0878. Or fax him at 919/733-4762.

THE RIGHT STUFF

There's a ton of techno-gear for telecommuters and home-office workers to choose from. Mainly, you're looking for equipment that's easy to transport, combines several capabilities, and doesn't take up too much space. Or, maybe you'd just like some cool stuff. Here's a sampling.

▶ OfficeJet. This neatly contained box is a combined ink-jet printer, plain-paper fax, and copier (full and reduced sizes). $959. Hewlett-Packard: 800/752-9000.

▶ PN60. A watch manufacturer has developed the smallest, most lightweight printer currently available. The one-pound device is laser-

quality with color capability using the optional color cartridge. $339. Citizen: 800/477-4683.

▶ Eris. This portable videoconferencing tool runs on a PC or Macintosh and includes a color camera and data base for storing the names, numbers, and even photos of your colleagues and clients. $5,000. RSI Systems: 800/496-4304.

▶ VideoMan. Now, you can conduct business face-to-face at a distance, using this color digital video camera for personal computer. Just set it next to your monitor and focus it on anything you'd like to broadcast to your videoconference cohorts. The VideoMan is OK for women, too. $279. Logitech: 800/231-7717.

▶ Adventure 4000. This gizmo will make callers think you have a big

operation. The 486 computer serves as a receptionist by answering the phone and taking messages. It can also transfer callers to any of 99 voice-mail boxes. Other capabilities include a fax and a speech-to-text function for remote retrieval of addresses and phone numbers. $2,000. AST Research: 800/876-4278.

▶ Ringmouse. The infrared, ultrasonic portable mouse is here. Wear it on your right or left index finger, point, and control your computer's cursor with the two buttons. $99. Spectrum/Kantek: 800/536-3212.

▶ AER Energy Power 220. This cube-thing is just the thing when your laptop or cell phone runs out of juice while you're on the run without any extra batteries. It works by a rechargeable zinc air cell that inhales oxygen and exhales electricity. $649. AER Energy Resources: 800/769-3720.

▶ CelDock. Just place your Motorola MicroTACH flip phone into the cradle and—presto!—a second phone line. It works like a regular phone line, except that calls are transmitted through the cellular network. The CelDock also recharges the phone's battery so it's ready to go when you are. $399. Telular Corporation: 800/636-3625.

After the beeper.... It's the age of the pager. Sophisticated versions now have small LCD screens that show numbers and messages (including e-mail) and notify you when you've received a fax or voice-mail message. Some page services will also forward faxes to you, such as FaxNow through PageNet. Two-way pagers on the horizon—such as Motorola's Tango—will acknowledge incoming messages with any of 120 programmed messages.

And look for Microsoft robot-builder Gordon Bell to create a videophone/laptop/camera that will serve as a link between home and on-site workers. Bell refers to this technology as "telepresence"—or "being there without really being there."

THE

FUTURE
at work

MANAGING THE FORCES THAT
ARE RESHAPING ORGANIZATIONS
AND OUR WORK LIVES

A planning tool for executives and human resource professionals

NOVEMBER–DECEMBER 93   ISSUE

M ANAGING THE INVISIBLE WORK FORCE
The opportunities of distributed work

6

To a significant degree, telecommunications and electronic technologies are making it possible for most people to work almost anywhere, and at any time. Managers and workers can operate effectively far away from the office and, in the future, will increasingly be doing so. The challenges of managing a work force that "isn't there" is what this issue is all about.

The culture of work is changing. People who were at their desks, who attended meetings, whose cars filled the parking lot, and who ate at the company cafeteria will in the future be mobile workers, working from home, on the road, at alternative sites, like hotels, airports, and customers' offices. It is possible that managers will be responsible for the work of people they have never seen, except on a video screen, or with people living on the other side of the country who show up for meetings once a year. The potential for distributing work away from the conventional downtown office is large and is only beginning to be explored.

Family and life-style pressures as well as the high cost of maintaining offices are forcing organizations to examine their basic assumptions about the nature of work. These pressures are accompanied by the orga-

nization's need for structural flexibility as worldwide competition gets stronger.

These changes are occurring at the same time as large organizations are moving to a smaller core of permanent workers, surrounded by a contingent work force that can be made to grow and shrink according to need. Although one might think that most of the distributed workers will be in the contingency ring, the new work arrangements will cut across all boundaries and include management. One reason is that favorable distributed work arrangements are often seen as a reward, and as an expression of the company's trust in an individual.

These rapidly evolving new work patterns are being driven by new technologies, including cellular telephones, portable office equipment, and convenient telecommunications data linkages. These technologies make it practical and attractive to work anywhere—in a customer's office, on a vendor's premises, in a hotel, on the road from a car or a van. Repair and maintenance workers, meter readers, route salesmen, company representatives, buyers, school board members, and farm agents can all be made independent of any central office for long periods by being suitably equipped with portable and electronic technologies that enable them to collect, record, and send information to the company's communication system.

Emerging technologies in personal communicators and locators will make it unnecessary for workers to sit in offices just so that others can find them when the demands of the work require that they be elsewhere. It is evident from the demographic characteristics of telecommuters, at least, that the maturing baby boomers, with an interest in flexible hours and workdays and in finding more time to spend with their families, are strong candidates for distributed work. Telecommuters today are likely to be 35 to 37 years old. Three-quarters of them are part of dual-income households with a median income of $40,000. About half have children under 18, and about a quarter have children under 6.[1]

Other drivers are the need to reduce costs of office space, to take the work closer to the customer, to respond to public policy interest in spreading the traffic load over the work day, and to reduce congestion and cut the commute to work to reduce air pollution. For example, the Clean Air Act requires companies with more than 200 employees in metropolitan areas to reduce their work forces' commuting mileage by 25% by 1996.

About 2 to 3% of the work force is now engaged in distributed work. By 2010, it will be about 20 to 25%.[2] Telecommuting is the most popular of the terms describing distributed work. About 2 million workers telecommute today, with about 7.5 to 15 million likely to be doing so in 2000.[3] Other terms are work-at-home, working in the electronic cottage, remote work, home-based work, and telework. They share a common feature in that the work is done away from the traditional central work location, and the results are increasingly likely to be delivered electronically. Beyond this, though, these terms call attention to particular aspects of the new work environment.

Telecommuting implies that the worker does part or all of the work with a computer and uses the telecommunications system to collect and deliver work, as well as to communicate with colleagues, supervisors, and customers. In effect, the work commutes, through phone lines and computers, but the worker does not. A telecommuter would most likely be working at home today. A likely trend will be the development of nearby telecommuting centers where a telecommuter can find the support technology he or she may need, such as copiers and advanced printing facilities, as well as a place to work.

Work-at-home has an obvious meaning, but it is also coming to mean people who rearrange their lives so as to do most of their work at home. Often, these are people who have their own businesses at home. A few examples—development and fundraising consulting, information brokers, litigation research, CPAs, house- and pet-sitting, writers, and editors—have all been developed as work-at-home businesses. Small businesses like these will increasingly be dependent on computers, telecommunications, and information technologies, but these are not necessarily the focus of their work.

Work in the electronic cottage is acquiring the meaning of getting away from it all, of being able to choose to live in an attractive rural community, and yet be connected to the fast-paced world of work without having to participate in it in person, to live a small-town life and be a worldwide player. While the emerging reality of distributed work may have some of these features, there are also gritty issues to be worked out, such as who does the cottager work for, how is the work to be managed, and how is it to be paid for.

Home-based work is often used to mean any work that can be done at home, such as machine knitting, word processing, craft work, and envelope stuffing. Unions oppose home-based work because they see opportunities for home-based workers to be exploited, as seamstresses used to be in the garment industry.

Telework can be done anywhere, at home, in a hotel, on the road. It can include telemarketing, phone sales, survey work, political canvassing, fundraising, and bill collecting. Teleworkers use the power of the telephone system to accomplish what advertising, direct mail, and door-to-door visits might have done in the past. And it can be fully automated, which means there may be fewer teleworkers in the future.

Not all of the distributed workers will be telecommuters. Some of them are, and will continue to be, briefcase workers, people who pack up some of their work and take it home to do. Jack Nilles of JALA International, Inc., an expert on telecommuting, found in 1985 that 70% of midlevel people, managers and professionals, were taking work home, and about 3% were telecommuting informally about one day a week. With more flexible work hours and work weeks becoming acceptable in the workplace, more of these briefcase workers will stay home additional days a week and bring a briefcase to the office for the work that has to be done there. The Conference Board found that about 80% of the companies they surveyed have informal telecommuters, and about 15 to 20% have formal arrangements for telecommuting.[4]

Experimental Telework Centers in California

A pilot project to set up ten neighborhood telecenters, where people can work within a walk or bicycle ride from their homes, is going on in California. Six or so people will go to work in each of the centers, no more than two of whom will be working for the same firm. The centers will be equipped with copying, fax, and communications facilities. This is a joint project that Jack Nilles is working on with CalTrans and the University of California at Davis, using funds from the U.S. Department of Transportation. U.S. DOT is currently exploring the transportation implications of distributed work.

EXPANDING THE USE OF DISTRIBUTED WORK

COMPANIES ARE LIKELY TO EXPAND THEIR USE OF DISTRIBUTED work in at least three ways: by formal programs, by tolerating and encouraging more informal telecommuting, and by using more contract workers who are likely to be self-employed professionals who make their own work arrangements and who deliver their results and get information through the organization's communications system.

The other expanding group of distributed workers will be those whose jobs have always taken them out of the office, route salespeople, for example. With more portable technology and electronic company networks that they can access on the road, they will need to spend little if any time at company offices. If they are repairpeople in fully equipped vehicles, they will be able to handle any data input and paperwork from their trucks. Instructions for the next day's work can be faxed to them at home, or downloaded to their home computers before they set out for the day. Items they use from the truck will automatically be debited from the truck's inventory. When they pick up new supplies, the automated warehouse will refill the inventory.

About 50% of distributed workers today work from one to three days a week out of the office, then work the remainder in the office or at another work site. Few work entirely at home. About 25% consider themselves telecommuters, but work less than eight hours a week at home.[5] This varied pattern is likely to continue for the next five to ten years as companies and people explore the possibilities of distributed work. It has been easier for smaller organizations to experiment with distributed work, particularly informal telecommuting. However, the use of distributed work is now growing most rapidly among large companies, those with more than 1,000 employees.

IMPROVED TECHNOLOGIES

SOME OF THE MOST USEFUL TECHNOLOGIES IN DEVELOPING distributed work programs have been around for years—the telephone, the fax machine, the copier, the personal computer, and videoconferencing. Improved capabilities in these technologies will be important, particularly in portability, power, lower costs, and ease of use. Connecting it all through electronic networks will accelerate the trend to distributed work by putting colleagues, projects, data bases, managers, and software tools no further than a fingertip away from the worker provided with a workstation and a power source. At present, many of the technologies are independent of one another, that is, the worker turns away from the computer screen to use the phone, gets up to send a report through the fax machine, goes down the hall to meet a colleague. In the future, the workstation will be able to send a fax, access a data base, handle a phone call, and maintain in one corner of the screen the image of a co-worker. As a

The Distribution of Telecommuting, by Size of Organization

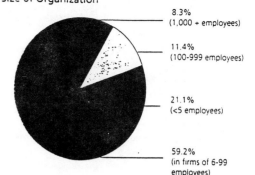

8.3% (1,000 + employees)

11.4% (100-999 employees)

21.1% (<5 employees)

59.2% (in firms of 6-99 employees)

Source: U.S. DOT, 1993, using Link Resources data

consequence, future workers will have to be reminded to take a walk or a break away from their work centers once in a while!

On the big, sprawling informal network, Internet, 1.5 million computers are already linked. Internet long since burst its U.S. boundaries and has expanded well beyond the scientific and university community where it began. The 1990s will be the decade of the network. On the future of networking, William R. Johnson, Jr., wrote, "In the 1990s, networking will evolve to the point where, for all practical purposes, people will be able to electronically communicate anything (voice, data, image, video) anytime, anywhere in the world."[6] He also believes that successful managers in the next ten years will be those who learn and understand how networking can expand their options, and what the technical, organizational, and economic trade-offs are in their use of networks.

Technology makes distributed work possible, but this is not the only important factor in its growth. There are several other underlying factors that will influence the decision to distribute work. One is the desire of employers to be leaner, faster, and more flexible in responding to business needs. The large corporation wants to be more like a small company, which is able to shift its human resources quickly to new tasks. With this goes a desire to shift the administrative and financial burden of a large permanent work force onto other, smaller companies that can then contract to supply a product or a service. In many cases, the contractor will be an individual worker who contracts to supply services on a temporary or permanent basis. This contractor makes his or her own arrangements about how and where to do the work.

Even with their permanent work forces, companies will be willing to experiment with distributed work to maximize productivity, and to reduce the costs of employment.

None of these work formats is entirely new, but they are moving from the perimeter to the center of the organization. They are becoming the rule, rather than the exception. As such, they will in the future be the norm for the manager, who must coordinate increasingly diverse work arrangements to achieve business goals.

SEEING THE EFFECTS OF DISTRIBUTED WORK ON THE ORGANIZATION

HE SHIFT TO DISTRIBUTED WORK IS CREATING GRADUAL CHANGE in organizations, as informal telecommuters become more formally accepted. As everyone becomes more accustomed to distributed work, one day it will become commonplace. Organizations will become virtual organizations, staffed by a work force of remote workers whose primary channels of communication are electronic, data, voice, and image. In this issue, however, we concentrate on what impacts management will encounter in the early stages of the distribution of work away from the central workplace, and how to prepare for the new work environments.

GROWTH OF DISTRIBUTED WORK WILL MEAN: 1. BROAD-SCALE REEVALUATION OF COMPANY RESOURCES

F 25% OF THE FUTURE WORK FORCE DOES NOT COME INTO THE office, what office space will a typical organization need? Less than today, obviously, but there may be a bigger question involved here. A typical company in the year 2000 could have the following distribution of workers:

Work force total:	5,000
At satellite centers	20%
Working from home	11%
At plants	40%
On-road distribution centers, branches	20%
Headquarters	9%

Old assumptions about office space, that everyone needed a desk and a space to work, are already obsolete. A few people will still need that space. The rest may have quite different needs that will drive the rethinking of work space for the organization as a whole. The New York advertising agency Chiat/Day, which has wholeheartedly adopted distributed work, is building a new center for distributed workers that is much more like a college's student union, or a clubhouse, than a traditional office. There will be lockers, access to equipment, a library, support facilities, a commons where distributed workers can eat and talk with others, project rooms that they can reserve for meetings, and so on. A more modest concept that today's companies are experimenting with, called *hoteling*, keeps a limited amount of office and meeting space open, and the off-site worker makes a reservation when he or she needs an office or wants to hold a meeting.

2. A NEW STYLE OF MANAGEMENT

ANAGERS MAY NOT REALIZE HOW THEIR OWN PRESENCE AND work habits influence those of the people who work for them, and how much each relies on the other for com-

ments and visual cues that communicate how the work is going, what the pace should be, and when it is okay to crack a joke and when it is wise to say nothing. Those managers whose style is to give commands face-to-face and see results will probably have the most difficulty in developing a new style that works well at a distance. All managers, probably, will benefit from some training in how to work effectively with people over the phone, through the computer, and by e-mail.

Managers may be reluctant to recognize that they must deliver more information, and more detail, on what needs to be done and why. Distributed workers, who are likely to work more on their own, will inevitably become more independent and more demanding of the information they need to turn in a good performance.

With close supervision of workers, trust is less important to managers. But the distance relationship will demand much more faith from managers. This may be difficult at first for managers who are used to trusting people who work for them. Jack Nilles makes the point, "Managers will learn that their people can do their jobs very well without supervision. It can be ego-deflating to realize this. But managers must become leaders rather than administrators. They decide what their people should be doing, give them the physical and intellectual tools to do the job, agree with them on the goals, and then get out of the way."

3. MORE CLEARLY DEFINED TASKS

HIS IS A NECESSARY OUTCOME OF THE DISTRIBUTED WORKER'S need to have more and better information at hand to complete the task. Since the worker at a distance will be less able to rely on informal chats and observation to gauge the relative importance of what he or she is doing, managers will have to provide clearly described work tasks, and discuss them carefully with the person assigned to do them. In this effort, the manager may have to clarify his or her own views on the importance of the work and its substance. This is likely to eliminate some unnecessary work and force manager and worker to take more care in matching their expectations. On the other hand, outcomes will become more important because the manager cannot walk by and look over the worker's shoulder and thus influence how the task is being done.

"A key to my continuing success has been the good fortune to work for supervisors who manage by result, not by proximity. Of course, I've made a special effort to protect my boss by providing information on my project status and work efforts regularly.... In this way not only does my boss know that I'm working, but he can relate to what I'm working on when questioned," says Bob Fischer, long-time telecommuter. This is an example of how an experienced person taught himself to work well with sympathetic managers. It may be more difficult for the average worker and manager to work out the details of communicating with each other. Each will have to learn and practice new skills. One practical way to do this is to

6
ISSUE

FUTURE SCAN WORKSHEET

MANAGING
THE INVISIBLE
WORK FORCE
*The opportunities
of distributed
work*

Here are some categories that you can use in your thinking about the potential opportunities for distributed work in your organization. The best way to approach this is to estimate rough percentages first, then use these to stimulate discussion with others.

1. CURRENT WORK SITES *(list them)*

Site	How Many Could Be Distributed? *(work at home, on the road, and so on)*	If We Built a Satellite Center?	What Would Make It Possible for More to Be Distributed?
Downtown HQ	3% do now, maybe 15% more could.	25%	Convincing their managers!

2. JOBS THAT HAVE SOME POTENTIAL FOR DISTRIBUTED WORK

	What Percentage Could Be Distributed?	What Would Make It Possible for More Work to Be Distributed?
Executives	95%	Training them in computer access so they can get the numbers they want
Managers		
Supervisors		
White-collar		
Blue-collar		
Administrative		
Clerical		
R&D		
Technicians		
Sales		
Receptionists		
Legal		
Other		

(Make your own additions to this list.)

build in a weekly or monthly reflection on the process that enables each to tell the other what worked well that week and what did not, and to decide mutually what other steps must be taken.

4. DOMINANCE OF ELECTRONIC COMMUNICATION

I T'S OBVIOUS THAT COMMUNICATION WITH the distant worker will be more electronic and less face-to-face, but it is perhaps not as obvious that the dominant mode of communication within and outside the organization will be electronic. Nilles, for example, notes that managers believe in the value of face-to-face communication but practice it less than they preach it, even when their people are within line of sight. So that as electronic communications become more general and easier to use, whole organizations will shift to doing business by phone, by network, by e-mail, by voice mail, and by videoconferencing. This benefits distributed work, but managers and workers will need training and practice in achieving and maintaining quality in their communications.

In earlier issues of *The Future at Work*, we discussed emerging technologies important to electronically based communication. One of the more underrated technologies, probably because of its high cost, is videoconferencing. Hourly costs for videoconferencing have fallen from about $2,000 in the early 1980s to as low as $15 today.[8] Businesses are likely to replace some travel and hold more frequent meetings by videoconference as the technology improves and grows more accessible. Videophones, video inserts on a workstation's monitor screen, and large, flat wall-screens are all emerging technologies that should make video communications more attractive and useful for distributed work. One most likely use will be to cut back the costs of bringing people to international meetings. For people around the world to meet at the same time, however, will require that some stay up late and others get up extremely early.

5. ACCESS TO A WIDER POOL OF TALENT

D ISTRIBUTED WORK WILL MEAN COMPANIES CAN HIRE THE BEST people, no matter where they live. Organizations are no longer limited to hiring only people who are willing to

---

Rank Xerox: An Example of Creating a Distributed Work Force

Rank Xerox, Ltd., in the UK, needed to reduce office overhead. Their solution was to create a new work arrangement for a group of workers. These workers, all professionals, were to contract from their homes to do the same work for the company they had been doing before, except that they were now free to take on other tasks for other companies. In effect, they were to become entrepreneurs or small businesspeople, although with a continuing tie to Rank Xerox.

Two Work Forces, Not One, Were the Result

In the process of setting up what was eventually to be a successful program, the company discovered it had two work forces, those it had dispersed to their own homes and businesses and those left behind. In retrospect, company managers wished they had paid more attention to the latter. The left-behinds faced a depleted work culture, with new tasks and responsibilities and the feeling that more attention and resources were being expended on the dispersed group than on them.

---

move or who live near enough to work in their offices. Nor do they have to lose a valuable person because his or her spouse gets a new job and must relocate, or because an individual has other reasons not to be able to come into the office to work. As well, it may become possible through distance work to acquire skills and training that a company would not otherwise be able to get through hiring. A potential high-value employee who can't, or won't, relocate could be brought on board as a distance worker.

6. END OF COMPANY CULTURE?

T HIS EXAGGERATES ANXIETIES ABOUT work that people are bound to feel. What will be left of the company culture if no one is there? The people you expect to see every day will not be there. The social exchanges with peers over coffee or across desks will be missing. Whom do you go to lunch with?

The people who stay in the office get some advantages: it is quieter, there are less interruptions, productivity goes up, and people tend to reorganize work to do it more efficiently. But the part of organizational culture that thrives on daily encounters will be diminished. This raises questions about loyalty, and the ability to build and maintain teamwork.

People will have other concerns about their work. Am I out of sight, out of mind? Will I not be considered for opportunities because I am not there? Will they forget to give me important information? When I go in for meetings, will I know anyone? Some people may miss the opportunity of socializing with other people at work, the chance of making friends, learning new skills from more experienced people, and of meeting a potential wife or husband.

Companies may find themselves having to create new work support groups, either electronically or in face-to-face meetings. In these groups, members can air experiences and issues around feeling isolated or forgotten by the organization. The groups can also be forums for sharing useful ideas, for training, and for orienting new members. In truth, many of us may have to let go our traditional assumptions about work relationships and what they involve. For example, many professional workers are already transferring their loyalty and their expectations of camaraderie and individual exchange to their peer groups and their professional associations. They no longer expect to satisfy all these needs at work.

THE COMMUNICATIONS WORKERS OF AMERICA'S GUIDELINES FOR TELECOMMUTING PROGRAMS

: Equal pay and benefits.

: Work to be done in the office for at least two days a week.

. No more than two visits a month to a telecommuter's home by a manager with 24 hours' notice in each case. *(Other management advice suggests managers should never visit workers' homes, because of the risk of harassment suits.)*

The company supplies equipment and materials and reimburses for higher utility and insurance costs. The union has the right to inspect home equipment for safety and ergonomics.

Telecommuters should see all routine job openings.

Employees must know if they are being monitored.

Training must be provided.

No one can be hired directly into a distributed job and must be able to end home-based work and return to the office.

Some managers will be talented and dedicated enough to preserve a strong culture among their distributed workers, and it will be important to morale and improving productivity that they do so. Management as a whole should look to fostering people's pride in contributing to the organization's products and services because of their quality, reliability, and integrity. Everyone should hear when the company does well, when customers praise it, and when it makes positive contributions to society. Distributed workers should get the opportunity to represent the company whenever possible, to customers, to their community, at training sessions, and at meetings. This will require that they be updated on the latest information about the business. When possible, distributed workers should have a direct channel to senior people for information.

7. NEGLECTED WORKERS?

ANK XEROX FORMED A SUPPORT GROUP FOR ITS TELECOMMUTERS (see box, p. 5). But it realized later that it should have also created a similar support group for those who still came to the office and felt left out of the new arrangements and unnoticed with all the attention given to the pioneering distributed workers.

Today, at least, the option of working at home—or, at any rate, out of the office—is seen as a reward, a perk. It's a sign that management trusts and has confidence in that individual. There may also be a feeling that the person is getting away with something—their contribution is so valuable that management will take it in any form. As well, the relationship of the workers still in the office with those who are working away from it will change. Those left behind may have to take on chores or support functions they did not have to do before. It will be important for managers to take the opportunity offered by the new arrangements to reorganize and enhance the work done at the office for the benefit and productivity of those who stay there.

Having said all this, it is definitely true that working at home or on the road is not for everyone. Many people go to work to get away from home. They want the contact with others and the security of an organized task every day. Prizing them away from their office desks could be difficult. They may not have a suitable place at home to work, or trust themselves to work well on their own. Building or leasing neighborhood work centers may be an acceptable and lower-cost option for managers and workers.

8. MANAGEMENT CHALLENGES

HERE IS NOT MUCH GUIDANCE AVAILable yet on the management of distributed work, and some companies have set up programs that attempt to maintain management control over time and task. While this may be reassuring to workers and managers, it is not likely to achieve the best results. These new workers and new work relationships need to have freedom to experiment and test for the best outcomes. In the next ten years, people who are experienced as distributed workers will themselves become managers, bringing more firsthand experience to the job. Management's biggest challenges, therefore, will be (1) educating itself about the options available in distributed work, including learning about the technology, the costs involved, and the systems needed to integrate distributed work, and (2) creating programs to take advantage of the opportunities that distributed work offers.

The expectations of the company, its current management practices, and its willingness to adapt to new circumstances will be critical to its success in distributing work. And for some individuals it will amount to abandoning familiar work patterns and blurring the clear lines between work life and home life. Given these problems and needs, expect to encounter resistance and foot-dragging from workers and managers.

Technology is not the problem, although companies will undoubtedly encounter technological barriers as they set up new programs. For example, ordinary phone lines, answering machines, faxes, and personal computers are sufficient for most distributed work, but some areas and communities do not yet have the telecom structure to handle high-speed data communication in telework centers.

Legal issues are not likely to be a problem either, except in some ambiguous situations such as zoning restrictions that limit the amount and kinds of work that can be done at home. Tax laws are currently not favorable to working at home, and state tax laws may come into effect when a company located in one state has employees in another. For example, an Indiana-based employer had to pay Ohio's corporate franchise tax because of one distributed worker who lived in

Ohio.[9] Withholding of state income taxes could also be increased when a company has distributed workers doing all or most of their work in other states.

The question of whether the distributed worker continues to be an employee or becomes an independent contractor comes up in the context of companies cutting back on their permanent work forces and outsourcing more of their needs. Aside from official status, the relationship between the company and distributed worker will evolve into one more like contract work than the traditional boss-employee relationship. But in at least a couple of cases, workers have sued to be regarded as employees, not as contractors, and therefore have the benefits of full-time employees, as well as the protection of the Fair Labor Standards Act.

Unions have been opposed to distributed work in general and home work in particular, anticipating exploitation. Recently, however, some unions are accepting the inevitability of new work styles and developing guidelines for fair treatment of distributed workers (see box, p. 6, for those developed by the Communications Workers of America). Their concerns could be an important issue for managers, but not likely to prevent implementation of distributed work programs.

9. A CHANGE IN MANAGEMENT POLICY

URING THE EARLY YEARS OF DISTRIBUTED WORK WHEN telecommuters are still the exception rather than the rule, managers can work out problems on a case-by-case basis. But as more people become involved and more of the organization's work becomes distributed, the need for change in management policy and practice will be more urgent and more widespread. Take productivity, for instance. Early reports are that telecommuters improve their productivity by anything from 12 to 50%.[11] But most of those who telecommute now are pioneers, people who have chosen to do so and are highly committed to showing their employers how successful they can be. When many more people do it, and some with less commitment to results, managers will have to think about how to achieve and maintain productivity gains from their invisible workers. As a result, managers are likely to become more involved in

Redesigning the work, work processes, and evaluation of results

Working out how to pay people for their results

Working on improving their own communication.

Jobs will be done differently from how they would have been done in the office. The process of working with others must be differently organized and managed. The question of how to pay for the work will come up, too. Distributed workers can still be paid based on their education, skills, and experience. But they can no longer be paid for their time. In a sense, when an employee came to work for an eight-hour day, management owned that worker's time. During the workday the manager could assign tasks, see when they were being carried out, and note when the employee was not being productive. That line-of-sight supervision of time disappears with the invisible worker. Distributed workers are now responsible for their own time management. Managers can only be concerned with results and be willing to pay more for outstanding outcomes. One of the advantages of no longer paying for time will be that, for managers, petty hassles with employees about lateness, slow returns from lunch, and personal phone calls on company time will all disappear.

Some fear that distributed workers will become isolated and less productive, lacking the daily contact with people that had sustained them at work. Eventually, with more distributed workers, people will work out their own solutions to this, but in the meantime managers may have to make special efforts to relieve isolation. Companies with formal programs of telecommuting are trying out newsletters for their invisible workers. Some managers bring their workers into the office weekly or monthly for face-to-face meetings.

The task of recruiting, hiring, and orienting a new person when 25 to 50% of the work force is distributed will present new challenges. How do you take the new person on a tour and introduce them to everybody? How can they even meet others?

Career planning will come up. It is almost inevitable that distant workers will suspect, correctly, that they are being passed over for the best assignments, for promotion, and for opportunities to take part in work-related events. It is likely that the invisible worker will miss some opportunities, but this may be a trade-off for more workday freedom that some are willing to accept.

There are also hundreds of nuts-and-bolts questions that will come up and may present issues to be resolved—the technology, for example. Who provides the computer equipment and pays for upgrading it? What is the company's

MANAGEMENT TIPS[10]

Teach (or arrange for training in) time management to distributed workers. Many of them will be working on their own for the first time. *It's important for people working at home to be able to resist the distractions of home, but you should also offer this training to those workers still in the workplace.*

Teach workers how to document their performance, using timesheets, status reports, weekly or monthly self-evaluations on progress, and so on. *This should not be done just for the manager's peace of mind but used as a tool for enhancing the person's ability to work independently.*

Encourage absent workers to use the company's e-mail and to make suggestions. *You may have to do some coaxing here.*

Supply, or ask them to get, the most sophisticated messaging system available. *However sophisticated, it must be easy to use and understand, or some of the benefits of communication will not be realized.*

responsibility for the safety, comfort, and security of an employee's home work space? Since this may be uncharted territory for many companies, managers will be well advised to put together a task force of managers, distributed workers, and technology people (as well as some of the people who will stay in the office) to work out the details.

WHAT YOU CAN DO TODAY

THE CHOICES OF HOW TO EXPLORE THE IMPLICATIONS OF THIS issue for your organization could well depend on how much distributed work is already going on in the company, and whether you have a source of information and experience in-house. If you don't, then you might be able to get some help from other companies, or from professional associations in HR and management, as well as consultants who are making a speciality of distributed work.

1. Locate a manager who has experience with distributed work arrangements and bring him or her in to talk with an interested management group.

2. Become acquainted with developments in the technologies that will support distributed work. Many of the publications in these areas are highly technical, but some of the easier reading ones are *The Office, Modern Office Technology, Information Week, Technology Review,* and *Training*. Also useful but more specialized are magazines like *Electronics Purchasing*. The U.S. Congress Office of Technology Assessment publishes reports on the state of the art of technologies as well as the policy and regulatory issues likely to arise. These can be bought from the Government Printing Office. The U.S. Department of Transportation is following distributed work for its potential effects on traffic patterns, and their reports are published through the GPO.

3. Poll your employees. How do they feel about distributed work?

References

1. U.S. Department of Transportation. *Transportation Implications of Telecommuting.* Washington, D.C.: U.S. GPO, 1993, p. 21.

2. Coates & Jarratt, Inc., estimate, 1992.

3. U.S. Department of Transportation. *Transportation Implications of Telecommuting.* Washington, D.C.: U.S. GPO, 1993, p. v.

4. Bob Filipczak. "Telecommuting: A Better Way to Work?" *Training*, May 1992, p. 54.

5. U.S. Department of Transportation. *Transportation Implications of Telecommuting.* Washington, D.C.: U.S. GPO, 1993, p. 12. Using data from Link Resources, 1991.

6. William R. Johnson, Jr., vice president, Telecommunications and Networks, Digital Equipment Corporation. "Anything, Any-
time, Anywhere: The Future of Networking." In Derek Leebaert (ed.), *Technology 2001: The Future of Computing and Communications.* Cambridge, Mass.: MIT Press, 1991, pp. 150–175.

7. Bob Fischer. "Confessions of a Corporate Telecommuter." *Work at Home.* Ameritech, Illinois Bell, 1993.

8. Joanie M. Wexler. "Electronic Meetings Increase." *Computerworld*, Feb. 18, 1991, p. 58.

9. Reported in U.S. Department of Transportation. *Transportation Implications of Telecommuting.* Washington, D.C.: U.S. GPO, 1993, p. 48.

10. Advice gleaned from *Work at Home*, the newsletter for home workers published by Illinois Bell. Our observations are in italics.

11. Jack Nilles. Based on managers' estimates.

The Future At Work
Managing the Forces That Are Reshaping Organizations
and Our Work Lives
Number 6, November–December 1993

produced by
COATES & JARRATT, INC.

The Future at Work (ISSN 1069-4951) is written and researched by the consulting firm of Coates & Jarratt, Inc., and published ten times a year by Jossey-Bass Inc., Publishers.
For each issue, JOSEPH F. COATES, JENNIFER JARRATT, and their team of researchers draw on wide-ranging sources, including scans of over 100 publications, reports, and daily newspapers; information from a variety of electronic data bases; and on their consultancy work orienting such companies as American Express, Merrill Lynch, Corning, and Hershey Foods to future studies.
Address editorial correspondence to COATES & JARRATT, INC., 3738 Kanawha St., N.W., Washington, DC 20015. (202) 966-9307

Researchers: JOHN MAHAFFIE, ANDREW HINES,
NINA PAPADOPOULOS
Managing Editor: MARTA MARETICH
Designer: MARILYN HILL

Published ten times per year
Subscription price is $249.00
To order:
call or write Jossey-Bass Inc., Publishers,
350 Sansome Street,
San Francisco, CA 94104, (415) 433-1767

Copying License Fees:
Jossey-Bass offers annual licensing agreements whereby paid subscribers may purchase the right to copy and distribute *The Future at Work*. The cost is $100 for up to fifty copies and $200 for any number above fifty copies. For information, please write or call Jossey-Bass Periodicals, (415) 433-1740.

Flexible Work Options

BEYOND 9 TO 5

BY ELIZABETH SHELEY

8:00 a.m. *Joe checks his voice mail while driving daughter Nina to school.*

9:02 *Joe runs six miles every morning.*

10:13 *Joe reads the paper before starting work.*

Workplace flexibility might strike some as old news, with flextime now almost as common as the coffee break. But as hard data on the subject begin to replace anecdotes, flexible work options are gaining strength both as a business imperative and as a new direction.

Retention has become a major reason behind workplace flexibility programs. As Joan Gardner, vice president of management resources at the DuPont Corp. in Wilmington, Del., says, "If we don't have programs that will encourage our people to stay, then somebody else is going to invent the next breakthrough product." And at the Big Six accounting firm of Deloitte & Touche LLP based in Wilton, Conn., Jim Wall, national director, human resources, is equally emphatic. "Our only competitive advantage is having talented people, so we need to keep them."

Another business argument for flexible work arrangements is that they allow companies to match the peaks and valleys of activity. More organizations have shifted their focus to how potential changes in schedule will affect the product. Reduced absenteeism, though often overlooked, is also a legitimate business rationale; flexible options not only strengthen commitment, but also give employees more time to handle the very situations that sometimes lead to absenteeism.

The message from those leaders trying out flexible options is: Focus on the business reason. If the work can get done and the employee pulls his or her weight, the employee on a flexible option will be more loyal and productive than other employees. By focusing on business concerns, the burden of equitable decision making—or playing favorites—is also eliminated. For example, not asking for the reasons behind flexible option requests leaves managers less vulnerable to having to judge whether one employee's baby is more important than another's elderly parent. HR managers at DuPont point out that corporate policy has never been to rank needs for flexible options, to pit child care against golf, or graduate study against writing poetry.

If employees—expecially managers—view the workplace flexibility program as an accommodation for people with special needs, they will not accept it as just another way of working. According to Marcia Kropf, vice president of research and advisory services at New York-based Catalyst, a nonprofit organization dedicated to effecting change for women, establishing programs is not enough to effect culture change. ⇨

PHOTOS, PHIL HUNTER

Employees must know about policies and be comfortable using the options. Dramatic shifts occur when the change is truly driven by senior management.

MOST POPULAR OPTIONS

Kropf points out that the most popular flexible options are those that involve the least change. Flextime and compressed work weeks, for example, call for the same number of hours, at the same workplace, as in traditional work arrangements.

Another popular option is telecommuting, which is gaining ground because of changes in technology that allow better communication with the office via e-mail, voice mail and other means. But this option, too, assumes full-time work. Since most workers want the money that comes with full-time hours, flextime and telecommuting are likely to remain the most commonly used—especially by men.

At White Plains, N.Y.-based Nynex, which provides phone service for the north-eastern United States, flexible work arrangements are viewed as a business impera-tive. According to Robyn Phillips, director of corporate culture initiatives, although women have shown a much stronger willingness to request flexible arrangements

11:09 *The laptop is a vital tool for Joe's work.*

12:05 p.m. *Joe has lunch with executives from a client company.*

1:20 *In the office, Joe presents data on the past fiscal year.*

that require approval, men use full-time flexible options such as compressed hours as often as do women.

Some employees worry about whether participation in an organization's flexible workplace program could make them more vulnerable in a downsizing. According to Kropf, it's a legitimate fear. "Those in flex options are seen as less committed, less loyal and less hard-working," she explains. "It's a very common concern."

Nynex's Phillips has looked at ways to combat this defeatist mentality. "When we find groups of employees who have an environment where flexibility can work, we discuss it with them, and promote it by giving examples of success" from within the company. Ultimately, it comes down to the relationship between the employee and the supervisor, however, and not all those relationships have the optimal level of trust. The Nynex HR department tries to show that productivity and loyalty improve when flexible work arrangements are available; where successful, they can promote the program more easily.

MANAGING EMPLOYEES USING FLEXIBLE OPTIONS

Workplace flexibility requires managers to develop a new set of skills. Managers used to manage by sight, and defined work by hours on site. If a worker was in the office for eight hours, the boss assumed that person did eight hours of work. But Kropf sees a need for new skills focusing on work flow, productivity and the nature of the work that needs to be done.

This has been the experience at Deloitte & Touche. Wall is convinced that most, if not all, of the 600 workers now on reduced hours would have left the company if it had not become more flexible. Deloitte & Touche's program was initiated by CEO J. Michael Cook, who was alarmed at the high attrition rate among the firm's female accountants. Interviews with employees, including some who left the organization, led to a flexible workplace program that solved the problem. To make the managers comfortable with the change and heighten awareness of related issues, the organization ran a mandatory two-day workshop on men and women as colleagues.

"We then had to create guidelines that were perceived as fair and communicate them broadly," said Wall. To prove that the new program could work, Deloitte & Touche called for volunteers to try the reduced hours program. Once they could show that the program worked, the HR department publicized it. Finally, they followed up with a survey and phone interviews of individuals using the flexible options.

The flexible workplace could have been a difficult issue without some creativity.

According to Wall, "Time is the principal avenue through which we make money." Employees must be willing to be flexible about flexibility; if an employee working an 80 percent schedule has to work on a Friday that is normally taken off, the time is made up elsewhere.

Trust, Wall says, is a big issue between the employee and supervisor. To illustrate, a manager working with Wall normally arrives between 7 and 7:30 a.m. and leaves about 10 hours later. "We don't even keep track," Wall explained. On a recent snow day, this manager put in a full day of work without coming in, routing calls to her home and getting as much or more work done as she would have on-site.

Wall points out that "we used to measure productivity by input rather than output." To measure the work product rather than the time somebody spends in the work station requires a change in mindset that may take some managers longer than others. Also, not all flexible work arrangements are appropriate for all people or all jobs.

2:35 *Joe writes a report for his boss about his lunch meeting.*

4:24 *Joe's wife, Erin, who starts work early, picks up Nina.*

4:45 *Joe examines data for a new project.*

FORMAL VS. AD HOC PROGRAMS

Many organizations have allowed employees to tailor their work schedules on an informal basis. The trend, however, is toward more formalized programs. Patricia

A DuPont MALE EMPLOYEE TOOK ADVANTAGE OF THE COMPANY'S FLEXIBLE OPTIONS TO CARE FOR HIS ILL SISTER; THEN ULTIMATELY TOOK LEAVE TO DONATE BONE MARROW TO HER.

Carson, director of people services, at United Air Lines (UAL), headquartered in Chicago, notes that when UAL became an employee-owned company in July 1994, the company formalized the flexible workplace in recognition of work/family issues. UAL set in motion employee involvement teams that addressed various issues; Carson led the employee task team that tackled the flexibility issue.

The team did focus groups, benchmarking and cost-benefit analysis. Once options were decided on, a human resource flexibility manual was developed, which provides guidance to working units that want to assess which flex options might work for them. Employees working at traditional desk jobs have shown the most interest in the 4/10 option (working four 10-hour days in a week) or the 9/80 option (working 80 hours in nine days of a two-week period).

"People want to reduce their days at work and reduce their commutes, but not their compensation," Carson explains. Now that UAL has seen these options work successfully, the company has begun experimenting with extending the 4/10 option to those workers whose jobs require round-the-clock coverage.

Similarly, Nynex has a written policy that describes the arrangements available, including guidelines on structuring and agreements, as well as how to evaluate the success of a particular option in the work unit.

5:47 *A visit to the dentist reveals no cavities.*

6:51 *Erin and Joe share a laugh while fixing dinner.*

8:00 *Daddy's bedtime stories are the best.*

KEEPING TRACK

In focus groups at Catalyst, employees using options more complicated than flextime often say that they want to know who else in their company is using the option, so they can discuss the best way to handle certain situations. Also, as Kropf explains, one of the best ways to promote an option is through internal examples of a similar situation that works.

"If HR managers are going to promote their workplace flexibility programs, they need to know who's doing what," she says. "When it is left up to the individual work groups to determine how flexible programs fit in their units—even with guidelines—the use of the options becomes very uneven."

More and more companies, however, are shifting the locus of control back to the work units. Cindi Johnson, senior work/life specialist at DuPont, explained that the company is moving from corporate HR dictating policy to letting the teams work out what they can and cannot manage in terms of flexibility and the needs of individual workers within those teams. Over all of this, however, is corporate guidance on such issues as cost neutrality and the need to keep business considerations first. To shift control to the work units, of course, presupposes healthy, functional teams. "Flexibility won't work in a dysfunctional team," Johnson says.

Like UAL, DuPont is attempting to adapt its workplace flexibility programs to its shift workers, who account for 80 percent of the company's employees. They have made it clear to the HR department that they want the day-to-day flexibility to address unforeseen needs and special events—to go to the dentist or watch a child in a school play, for example. According to Johnson, when jobs must be covered 24 hours a day, seven days a week, flexibility has to be handled differently—and there may actually be more opportunity for flexibility. DuPont already has some job-share partners on assembly lines, and other types of flexible programs are in place.

At Nynex, with 62,000 employees, Phillips believes it would be a daunting task to track the entire organization. Instead, tracking takes place at one of the work units, and is interpolated forward to the rest of the company.

FUTURE PROGRAM EXPANSIONS

At Nynex, Phillips sees that acceptance of workplace flexibility goes hand-in-hand with greater workforce diversity. As both flexibility and diversity have grown into strategies for productivity, Nynex has expanded its efforts to create stronger, broader programs. The company has had unexpected success with its gradual return-to-work program. Developed between the union and management, this program allows individuals on family leave to return to work on a part-time basis over time. Nynex found that employees will return sooner if they have the flexibility to adjust their hours.

DELOITTE & TOUCHE MANAGERS REALIZED THEY WERE LOSING WOMEN ACCOUNTANTS AFTER SEVEN OR EIGHT YEARS OF EMPLOYMENT AT THE COMPANY—THEREFORE LOSING THEIR INVESTMENT IN THOSE EMPLOYEES. SENIOR MANAGEMENT DECREED THAT THE COMPANY FIND OUT WHY THIS WAS HAPPENING AND STOP IT, WHICH LED TO THE DEVELOPMENT OF THE FLEXIBLE WORKPLACE PROGRAM.

EIGHT STEPS

Introducing a Workplace Flexibility Program

Barney Olmstead and Suzanne Smith, co-directors of the San Francisco-based consulting firm, New Ways to Work, and co-authors of *Creating a Flexible Workplace: How to Select and Manage Alternative Work Options*, outline the following eight steps for introducing a new scheduling or staffing option:

1. **Gain support for the program.** A system of ongoing dialogue is key to educating both management and workers about the reasons for the change.

2. **Set up the program's administration.** One person should oversee implementation of the program's details, ensuring that technical assistance is provided for supervisors and employees.

3. **Design the program.** Verify that current policy is compatible with the new objectives. Olmstead and Smith recommend addressing issues such as eligibility, an application process, effect on employee status, and reversibility.

4. **Develop resource materials for both employees and supervisors.** These should include a program description, educational and technical assistance materials, training where necessary, and other support and guidance, with the goal of having workers and managers who are well-informed.

5. **Announce the program.** This may seem obvious, but some companies have waited for employees to ask if certain workplace options are available.

6. **Promote the program.** Especially when the concepts involved are unfamiliar, employees will benefit from knowing that participation in workplace flexibility programs will not have a negative effect on their career hopes or earning potential.

7. **Evaluate the program.** Ask if it has had the desired effect, and if not, why not. Examine the financial ramifications, problem areas, unexpected benefits, and employee and supervisor reactions.

8. **Fine-tune the program.** The evaluation process will provide at least some of the information necessary to make the adjustments that will make a workplace flexibility program of optimum benefit to both the company and its employees.

For more information on flexible work options and a glossary of terms, see HRMagazine, February 1994 cover package starting on page 42. Also, see HRMagazine's section on the SHRM web page, http://www.shrm.org/hrmagazine.

In addition, the organization is actively promoting telecommuting, and not just because it's a telephone company. The science and technology unit lacks sufficient office space; when its workers began telecommuting, that problem was automatically solved, thus meeting a business need. Having recently revamped its policy in consideration of the Clean Air Act, among other issues, Nynex is now conducting pilot programs in telecommuting among its employees.

Employees at Deloitte & Touche were telecommuting before anyone ever knew what it was, suggests Wall. "A lot of our work was already off site, on the road, in hotel rooms, in airplanes, in the clients' offices." He sees this increasing, especially since he believes that use of flexible options leads to the desire to use the options—in other words, as more people become comfortable with an option, others will experiment with it, too.

According to Wall, productivity goes up once flexible options are in place, and the return on investment is immediate. He advises companies seeking to establish or expand their programs to understand why they need the program, to communicate broadly, and to be willing to experiment "and therefore fail" once in a while. DuPont's Johnson often gets calls from other companies: "I tell them not to ask me, to ask their own employees. That's what we did." Back in 1985, DuPont started by asking employees what they wanted. Every policy and program now in place is one the employees sought. 🖪

9:30 *Back on-line with the office, Joe thinks about the new account.*

Elizabeth Sheley is acting managing editor for HRMagazine.

THE FACTS

Hard Data from DuPont

"When I started working at DuPont, I was told 'leave your personal life at home and your work life at the office.' Well, we've learned that's impossible," said Ed Woolard, departing CEO of DuPont.

DuPont first did research on child-care issues in 1985. By 1995, the company had 10 years of data indicating that use of flexible options is a good business practice in and of itself. While establishing its workplace flexibility programs, the company has been emphatic that business needs must be met before all other considerations. But DuPont now has data indicating that the workplace flexibility program presents a strategic benefit.

In October 1995, DuPont released a study documenting the correlation between employee commitment to business success and the company's workplace flexibility programs. The study of some 18,000 employees from nearly 20 business units provides a 10-year comparison with the results from two previous studies.

The results of the study clearly indicate that work/life programs are a powerful tool to motivate people and encourage commitment to achieving business objectives," said John A. Krol, DuPont president and CEO-designate.

The survey showed employees using or aware of the DuPont workplace flexibility program to be the most committed employees in the company, and the least likely to feel overwhelmed or burnt out. They were 45 percent more likely than those not using the services to strongly agree that they will expend extra effort on the company's behalf. An additional 33 percent were more likely to report feeling supported by the company. With an average reported work week of 47 hours (55 hours per week for managers) the study found no difference in work hours reported between those with and without dependent-care responsibilities.

The survey also found that 41 percent of DuPont's employees have used flexible hours, 6 percent have worked as telecommuters, 4 percent have used family leave, and 3 percent have reduced their hours. But employees are still making tradeoffs to achieve a balance between their work and family obligations: 34 percent will not accept relocation, 24 percent would refuse jobs with increased travel, 21 percent would refuse jobs with more stress or overtime, and 12 percent have refused promotions.

FURTHER READING

Compiled by Linda M. McFadden

The Virtual Workplace, Telework, Telecommuting, Home Offices (1994-present)
Alternative Officing and Work Strategies

Institute for the Future. "The Best of Times, the Worst of Time: Income Distribution in the Knowledge Economy." *Rethinking the Workplace*. Menlo Park, CA: Institute for the Future, 1995: 223-228.

Chartrand, Sabra. "Home Office: Learning to Work Where You Live." *The New York Times* May 5, 1996.
(http://www.nytimes.com/web/docsroot/library/jobmarket/0505sabra.html)

Collaborative Strategies. "Electronic Collaboration on the Internet and Intranets." Collaborative Strategies, 1996. (http://www.collaborate.com)

"Evolutionary Workplaces." Zeeland, MI: Herman Miller, Inc. 1996.

"Future Work." *Fast Companies* August:September 1996: 55-56.

Grenier, Ray, and George Metes. *Going Virtual: Moving Your Organization into the 21st Century*. Upper Saddle River, N.J.: Prentice Hall, 1995.

Hylton, Richard D. "The Revolution in Real Estate." *Fortune* September 5, 1994: 94-98.

Institute for the Future. "Mapping the Future of the Virtual Office." *Rethinking the Workplace*. Menlo Park, CA: Institute for the Future, 1995: 205-213.

Nilles, Jack M. *Making Telecommuting Happen: A Guide for Telemanagers and Telecommuters*. NY: Van Norsand Reinhold, 1994.

Rheingold, Howard. *The Virtual Community*. San Francisco: Harper, 1993. (Also available free on the Internet at www.webcom.com/~pcj/it-nf/itn-078.html)

Tapscott, Don. *The Digital Economy*. New York: McGraw-Hill, 1996.Telecommuters. New York: Van Nostrand Reinhold, 1994.

Trent, James R., Amy L. Smith and Daniel L. Wood. "Telecommuting: Stress and Social Support." *Psychological Reports* 1994, 74: 1312-1314.

Turkle, Sherry. *Life on the Screen: Indentity in the Age of the Internet*. New York: Simon & Schuster, 1995.

Turkle, Sherry. *The Second Self: Computers and the Human Spirit.* New York: Simon & Schuster, 1984

Institute for the Future. *"Work+Family+Information Technology=???"* Menlo Park, CA: Institute for the Future, 1995: 215-222.

The Changing Nature of Work

Becker, F., and M. Joroff. *Reinventing the Workplace.* Norcross, GA: International Development Research Council, 1995.

Fox, Matthew. *The Reinvention of Work.* San Francisco: Harper Collins, 1995.

Jones, Michael. *Creating an Imaginative Life.* Berkeley CA: Conari Press, 1995.

Korten, David C. *When Corporations Rule the World.* San Francisco: Berrett-Koehler, 1995.

Rifkin, Jeremy. *The End of Work.* New York: G.P. Putnam's Sons, 1995.

Schrage, Michael. *No More Teams! Mastering the Dynamics of Creative Collaboration.* New York: Currency Doubleday, 1996.

Web sources:

Furniture industry-

Haworth Co. Home Page: http://www.haworth-furn.com
> Provides customer oriented information on real estate facilities planning and design. Includes the following as of August, 1996:

> "How to Increase Productivity Through Teamwork"

> "Overview and Glossary of Alternative Officing Concepts," by Chak Bautista and Martha Whitaker, Hellmuth, Obata and Kassabaum, Inc. (HOK), *Office Journal 9*

> "Telecommuting," by Ken Robertson, KLR Consulting Inc., *Office Journal 10*

> "New Ways to Work: Hoteling and Homework," Beth Harmon-Vaughan, HNTB Corp., *Office Journal 12*

> "Work Trends and Alternative Work Environments"

> "Case History: Creating a Team Environment," by Marilyn Heit, National Demographics & Lifestyles/The Polk Company, *Office Journal 12*

Herman Miller, Inc. Home Page: http://www.hmiller.com.

Steelcase Co. Home Page: http://www.steelcase.com

Other-

About Work: http://www.aboutwork.com

Bell Atlantic's LBS Enterprise Exchange: http//www.bell-atl.com/conf/lbs/entrexch

Collaborative Strategies: http://www.collaborate.com

Conway Data, Inc.: http://www.conway.com

Electric Minds: http://www.minds.com

Facilities Design and Management: http://www.fdm.com/

Gil Gordon Associates: http://www.gilgordon.com/us.html

Info-Tech Guide: http://www.webcom.com/ ~ pcj/it-nf/

Institute for the Study of Distributed Work:
http://www.dnai.com/ ~ isdw/Bibliography.html

The Smart Valley Telecommuting Guide:
http://smartone.svi.org/PROJECTS/TCOMMUTE/TCGUIDE/

Telecommute America: http://www.att.com/Telecommute_America

Telecommuting Advisory Council: http://www.telecommute.org/

Telecommuting and Telework Resource Page:
http://grove.ufl.edu:80/ ~ pflewis/commute.html

Telecommuting and Travel Resource Page: http://www.engr,ucdavis.edu/ ~ its/telecom/
Telecommuting Tips, Pacific Bell: http://www.pacbell.com/

The Virtual Workplace: http://www.cgs.edu/ ~ igbariam/chapter.html/

Associations (in addition to those listed as sites above)

International Development Research Council (IDRC)

International Facility Management Association (IFMA)

Organizational Development Theory, Teamwork

Bass, Lawrence W. *Management by Task Forces*. Mt. Airy, Maryland: Lomond Books, 1975.

Camevale, Anthony Patnch. *America and the New Economy: How New Competitive Standards are Radically Changing American Workplaces*. San Franscisco: Jossey-Bass, 1991.

Fisher, Kimball. *Leading Self=Directed Work Teams: A Guide to Developing New Team Leadership Skills*. NY: Mc Graw-Hill, Inc.

Galbraith, Jay R., & Edward E. Lawler. *Organizing for the Future: The New Logic for Managing Complex Organizations*. San Francisco: Jossey-Bass, 1993.

Goodman, Paul S., and Associates. *Designing Effective Work Groups*. San Francisco: Jossey-Bass, 1992.

Heckman, Richard J. ed. *Groups that Work (and Those That Don't)*: Creating Conditions for Effective Teamwork. San Franscisco: Jossey-Bass, 1992.

Hampden-Turner, Charles and Alfons Trompenars. *The Seven Cultures of Capitalism: Value Systems for Creating Wealth in the United States, Japan, Germany, France, Britain, Sweden, and The Netherlands*. New York: Doubleday, 1993.

Jacobs, Robert. *Real Time Strategic Change*. San Francisco: Berrett-Koehler, 1994.

Johansen, Robert, et al. *Leading Business Teams: How Teams Can Use Technology and Group Process Tools to Enhance Performance*. New York: Addison-Wesley, 1991.

Katzenbach, Jon R., and Doublas K. Smith. *The Wisdon of Teams: Creating the High Performance Organization*. Cambridge: Harvard Business School Press, 1993.

Larson, Carl E., and Frank M.J. LaFasto. *TeamWork: What Must Go Right/What Must Go Wrong*. Newbury Park: Sage Publications, 1989.

Loehr, Linda C. *Communication Processess in Cross-Functional Project Teams: A Case Study*. Ann Arbor, MI: UMI Dissertation Services, 1990.

Orsburn, Jack D., et al. *Self-Directed Work Teams: The New American Challenge*. Homewood: Business One Irwin, 1990.

Parker, Glenn M. *Team Players and Teamwork: The New Competitive Business Strategy*. San Francisco: Jossey-Bass, 1991.

Renesch, John, editor. *Leadership in a New Era*. San Francisco: Sterling & Stone, 1994.

Sundstrom, Eric, and Irwin Altman. "Physical Environments and Work-Group Effectiveness." *Research in Organizational Behavior* 1989: 175-209.

Sundstrom, Eric, et al. "Work Teams: Applications and Effectiveness." *American Psychologist* February 1990: 120-133.

Weisbord, Marvin R., et al. *Discovering Common Ground*. San Francisco: Berrett-Koehler, 1992.

Weisbord, Marvin R. *Future Search*. San Francisco: Berrett-Koehler, 1995.

Weisbord, Marvin R. *Productive Workplaces: Organizing and Managing for Dignity, Meaning and Community*. San Francisco: Jossey-Bass, 1990.

Wheatley, Margaret. *Leadership and the New Science*. San Francisco: Jossey-Bass, 1992.